folk

Characters and events in the history
of
Bedfordshire and Northamptonshire

Vivienne Evans

with line drawings by
Joan Schneider

The Book Castle

To
Barry Stephenson, County Special Collections
Librarian, and his Staff.

First published October 1989
by
The Book Castle
12 Church Street
Dunstable
Bedfordshire LU5 4RU

Reprinted October 1994
with the aid of sponsorship by
Aerospace Composite Technologies
London Luton Airport

ISBN 1 871199 25 5

Printed and bound by
Antony Rowe Ltd., Chippenham

Cover features two photographs of
'Past Times in Good Company' – a
touring musical group from Los Angeles, USA,
performing at Holdenby House, Northants.

CONTENTS

(B) Bedfordshire   **(N) Northamptonshire**

INTRODUCTION

During the many years that I have been carrying out research in the Local History Collection of the Bedford Central Library (Harpur Street) or elsewhere, I have returned over and over again to the bound volumes of 'The Bedfordshire Magazine', 'Northamptonshire Past and Present', the publications of the Bedfordshire and Northamptonshire Record Societies and 19th century copies of 'The Bedfordshire Times'. Whatever stories I have been researching, there has always been an even more fascinating story on the facing page! Equally, whenever I go into the County Record Offices with a list of references, I never complete my list because I am sidetracked by the tantalising stories that I see entered in the catalogues.

When I first started researching local history, there were a handful of major books covering the history of each county. Now our libraries have shelves full of books and booklets covering the history of numerous towns and villages in each county, and carefully researched and presented histories of churches, schools and local customs.

For some years now I have longed to have an opportunity to stop to read these stories and articles, and where possible to research them just that bit further. I am, therefore, extremely grateful to our publisher, Paul Bowes, for giving me the opportunity to do just that. This book is made up of around a hundred and fifty stories – all about people; young and old, rich and poor, famous and unknown, alive today or dead for nearly a thousand years.

Aware as I am of the great and growing interest in family history, and the circumstances under which our ancestors lived, the names of the people whose events form this book have been indexed separately.

The people and stories of which this book is made up are a personal selection, chosen to offer as wide and interesting a picture as possible. Undoubtedly, many people will feel disappointed that their favourite local story has been left out, for which I am sorry, but the books and magazines mentioned above are still in regular production and in many cases back numbers are available. The staff of our local libraries will be pleased to guide readers towards further sources of this kind of story.

Through the years I have had cause to be extremely grateful to the staff of all local libraries and archives but on this occasion I would like to give a special thank you to Barry Stephenson and his staff at the Local History Collection Bedford, without whose help this book would not have been possible.

I would also like to thank those friends who suggested suitable stories, such as the ancestor of one of the rioting church wardens of Elstow; Adèle Kane, who has driven me to and fro across the two counties and helped with the research; Marlene Pothecary who once again has repeatedly typed and retyped at a moment's notice and Joan Schneider whose inspired drawings are such a delightful part of this book.

Map of Bedfordshire

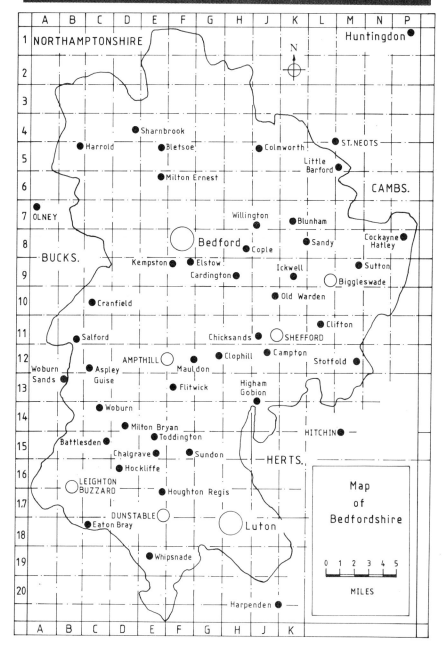

	A	B	C	D	E	F	G	H	J	K	L	M	N	P
1	NORTHAMPTONSHIRE											Huntingdon		

NORTHAMPTONSHIRE

N

Huntingdon

Sharnbrook

Harrold   Bletsoe   Colmworth   ST. NEOTS

Little Barford

Milton Ernest

CAMBS.

OLNEY

Willington   Blunham

BUCKS.   Bedford   Cople   Sandy   Cockayne Hatley

Kempston   Elstow

Cardington   Ickwell   Sutton

Biggleswade

Cranfield   Old Warden

Clifton

Salford   Chicksands   SHEFFORD

AMPTHILL   Clophill   Campton

Maulden   Stotfold

Woburn Sands   Aspley Guise   Flitwick   Higham Gobion

Woburn

Milton Bryan   HITCHIN

Battlesden   Toddington

Chalgrave   Sundon   HERTS.

Hockliffe

LEIGHTON BUZZARD   Houghton Regis   Map of Bedfordshire

DUNSTABLE   0 1 2 3 4 5
Eaton Bray   Luton   MILES

Whipsnade

Harpenden

x

Map of Northamptonshire

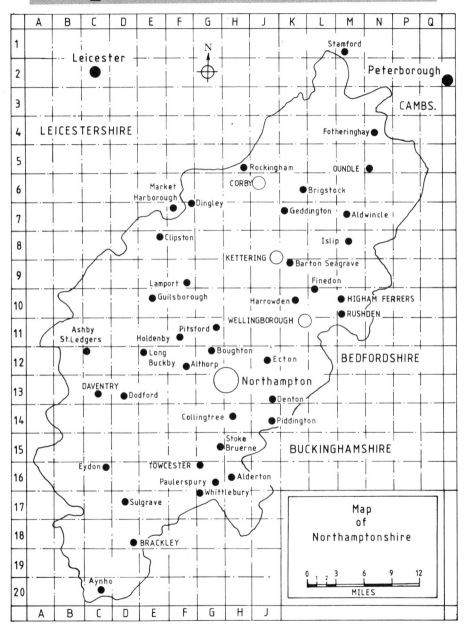

	A	B	C	D	E	F	G	H	J	K	L	M	N	P	Q

1

Stamford

Leicester
N

2
Peterborough

3
CAMBS.

4 LEICESTERSHIRE
Fotheringhay

5
Rockingham · OUNDLE

6 Market · CORBY
Harborough · Brigstock

7 · Dingley
Geddington · Aldwincle

8 · Clipston
Islip

9 KETTERING
Barton Seagrave

Lamport · Finedon

10 · Guilsborough
Harrowden · HIGHAM FERRERS

11 Ashby
St.Ledgers · Pitsford
WELLINGBOROUGH · RUSHDEN

Holdenby

12 · Long
Buckby · Boughton
Althorp · Ecton
BEDFORDSHIRE

13 DAVENTRY · Dodford
Northampton
Denton

14 Collingtree · Piddington

15 Stoke
Bruerne
BUCKINGHAMSHIRE

16 Eydon · TOWCESTER · Alderton
Paulerspury

17 Sulgrave · Whittlebury

Map
of
Northamptonshire

18 · BRACKLEY

19
0   1   2   3   6   9   12

20 Aynho
MILES

	A	B	C	D	E	F	G	H	J

Alderton

AN UNUSUAL ARREST

Sometime around 1600, the village constable, Richard Butler, received a message from the High Commissioner's Office, in London. He was to arrange the arrest of a man called John Simpson, who appears to have been accused of adultery by the church court.

Simpson was lodging with a widow in the village, so the constable visited a magistrate, collected a warrant and, accompanied by one of the magistrate's servants (who was armed with a pistol), went to the widow's house, in the middle of the evening, when he was quite confident that Simpson would be at home. He read out the arrest warrant and tried to carry out the arrest, but Simpson refused to come out of the house. Rightly or wrongly, the servant went in with his pistol, and tried to force an arrest. However, he wasn't quick enough, Simpson grabbed the pistol, and, in the confusion, the servant was shot dead.

Simpson was taken to the Assizes at Northampton and accused of murder, where he claimed it was not murder but self-defence. Because his original 'crime' was only recognized in the church court, the magistrate's servant had not had the legal right to use a pistol when arresting him.

After much legal debate the judges agreed with him and Simpson was released.

Aldwincle

A RESTORATION POET AND HIS RIVAL

John Dryden, the famous poet, was born here in 1631. He so dominated the literary scene of his time that it is sometimes referred to as the 'Age of Dryden'. He attended Westminster School around 1644, and entered Trinity College Cambridge in 1650 obtaining a BA degree four years later.

His longest poem, Annus Mirabilis, published in 1667, commemo rated two victories at sea by the English navy and the ending of the war with Holland, the long-awaited ending of the plague, which caused so many deaths in 1665, and the recovery from the Great Fire which had devastated London in 1666. He was appointed Poet Laureate in 1668, and held the position during the reigns of Charles II and his brother James.

Dryden, like the majority of poets of the 17th century, relied on financial support from his patrons, so that several of his works are written with the definite intention that they would be presented to the subject of the poem, or to their friends and supporters. In 1659 he published some verses on the death of Oliver Cromwell and in 1660 'A Poem on the Happy Restoration and Return of His Sacred Majesty Charles The Second'. Throughout his adult life he produced twenty-two plays, few of which are performed today, although 'Marriage à la Mode' is still well-known to students of Restoration drama.

For a few years, around 1680, Elkanah Settle, who was born at The Nags Head Inn, Dunstable, in February 1648, was a rival of Dryden, both competing for theatres and patronage. In 1682, Dryden made fun of Settle in his 'Absalom and Achitophel' while Settle produced 'Absalom Senior, or Achitophel Transpros'd'. The sparring continued for a few years but gradually Settle's work received less and less popular support.

He was seventeen years younger than Dryden and when the latter died on 1 May 1700 and was buried in Westminster Abbey, Settle must have hoped to take on his role of popular and respected author. During the 1690's he was City Poet and on numerous occasions produced 'The Triumphs of London', a series of pageants to be produced at the Lord Mayor's Show. He continued as a playwright during the first eighteen years after Dryden's death, but had no great success as a dramatist and financially he became so poor that his friends arranged for him to live as a pensioner in the London Charterhouse. He died there on 12 February 1724.

Althorp

PRINCESS DIANA'S ANCESTRAL HOME

Althorp House was originally built by Sir John Spencer in the early 16th century, but in 1768 Henry Holland was invited to redesign it and made such major alterations that it is now a handsome 18th century house. Queen Elizabeth visited the original house in 1603 and created Sir Robert, Baron Spencer. The family were ardent Royalists and throughout the centuries were close friends and advisers to the English Royal Family. Lady Diana's grandmother, Lady Cynthia Spencer, was Lady of the Bedchamber to the present Queen Mother.

Lady Diana's grandfather, the seventh Earl Spencer, lived at Althorp until his death in 1975, so for the early years of her life she lived with her parents, two older sisters and younger brother at Park House, Sandringham (Norfolk). She was born on 1 July 1961 and was christened at St. Mary Magdalene, Sandringham. Her parents were divorced in 1969 and when her grandfather died in 1975, her father, who had become the eighth Earl Spencer, moved with his son and daughters into Althorp House. Diana, who now for the first time took the title 'Lady Diana', was nearly fourteen years old.

ROMANCE AT ALTHORP

Although Lady Diana and her brother and sisters had frequently played with the royal children during their Christmas visits to Sandringham, she was much younger than Prince Charles and knew him less well than his younger brothers. In her teens she was still away at school at the time that her older sister, Lady Sarah, was often seen out with parties of young people, which included Prince Charles. However, during November 1978 she had permission to return to Althorp and take part in a house party arranged by her father and his new wife, Raine Countess of Dartmouth, daughter of romantic novelist Barbara Cartland. Prince Charles was there as the guest of Lady Sarah. There were far too many guests for him to notice Lady Sarah's young sister at the grand dinner on the Sunday evening, but on the following morning, out in the Althorp fields, near Nobottle Wood, Lady Sarah introduced them. From this chance meeting in the Northamptonshire countryside their friendship blossomed. Two years and three months later they became engaged, and were married at St. Paul's Cathedral on 29 July 1981.

Ampthill EF12

THE PROFESSOR OF AMPTHILL

Early Career

Sir Albert Richardson, President of the Royal Academy in 1955 and 1956, was born in Hampstead in 1880. At fifteen he was articled to Victor Page, an architect who had his offices in Gray's Inn Road and he also attended evening classes at Birkbeck College to study Building Construction and Design. By the time he was 25 he had moved around to work with other, carefully chosen architects and had a wide experience of both ecclesiastical, civic and domestic buildings.

It was not until August 1917 that he made his first recorded visit to Ampthill. The previous year he had joined the Royal Flying Corps as a second lieutenant. Having spent some time at the School of Military Aeronautics at Reading, he was about to be moved to a more physically demanding job so decided to undertake a long day's march to improve his fitness. By this time he had married and was the proud father of an eight year old daughter. They were living in an eighteenth century house in London Road, St. Albans and so, with a friend, he caught an early morning train to Bedford intending to march back. However, their march was interrupted several times as Richardson spotted first one and then another elegant building which had previously been unknown to him. When they reached Ampthill, his excitement brought their march to an abrupt halt – the church, the marketplace, the Georgian houses – all had to be recorded in detail. One red-brick house in Church Street particularly inspired him and he promised himself that once the war was over, he would return and buy it for his family, and that is exactly what he did.

In March 1919 he was appointed Professor at the Bartlett School of Architecture, University College, London and shortly afterwards, editor of 'The Architect's Journal'. His career as one of the foremost architects of this century, his important work in restoring many of the historic buildings damaged during the war, his influence in balancing the modern, extreme architectural enthusiasm of the post-war school of architects with the classical lines of the dignified, lasting beauty of the designs from previous centuries, have all been recorded by his grandson Simon Houfe in a fascinating book called 'Sir Albert Richardson – The Professor'.

The Eccentric Professor

The many people in Ampthill and round about, who remember the Professor, will recognise, within the pages of the above book, the man whose love of Georgian England in general and Ampthill in particular, carried him over the edge of eccentricity. His wild enthusiasms would lead him to stride into a house, ignore the owner and lovingly stroke a piece of furniture that had caught his eye, or would result in him greeting a shopkeeper not by complimenting him on his window display but on the quality of his window frames. When the Richardsons arrived in Ampthill the local gentry left their visiting cards and invitations to share their polite afternoon teas or other entertainments. While Mrs. Richardson balanced her tea cup and tried to concentrate on the conversation, her husband prowled around the drawing rooms and studied the undersides of furniture.

The Right Man At The Right Time

After the War, Richardson's experience of historic buildings was called upon over and over again to help restore or replace damaged buildings. Government departments, The Church Commissions, civic authorities and private individuals asked his advice about major constructions and minute details. Ampthill Rural District Council asked him to design and draw up plans for a model housing scheme. This delighted him as it gave him the chance to plan seven-roomed houses, with well-fitting sash windows and panelled front doors, at a price that the council could afford. Each one had a garden and they were placed around a green to give the feeling of a community or village.

The Pregnant Penguins

Throughout the 1950's Richardson held important positions both in education and in the commercial world of art and architecture. His two years as President of the Royal Academy were the climax of many previous honours. Whatever he undertook, however long he was obliged to stay in London or elsewhere, he always looked forward to his return to Ampthill. Regardless of the domestic inconvenience he kept his Church Street house just as it was when it was built in the 1780's and he furnished it with the utmost care. In every way possible and often at his own expense he tried to prevent anything being done that would damage the Georgian street scenes of Ampthill. On several occasions other towns and cities invited or commissioned him to advise on the difficulties of adding modern conveniences to their historic towns. Therefore, Richardson was at first hurt and later horrified when, without telling him, Ampthill Urban District Council decided to install new lamp posts alongside the Georgian buildings. When he discovered that these would not only be made of concrete but would be thirty feet high he tried everything possible to stop them. The media took up the story and gave it a great deal of publicity. Richardson himself described them as 'just like attenuated concrete penguins' and from this the press

5

AMPTHILL (contd)

coined the popular title of 'Pregnant Penguins'. Although the arguments became very bitter, the council refused to alter their plans.

Memorials

The Professor lost the battle of the lamp posts but it would be terrible to end this story on a negative theme. His post-war work which was responsible for restoring so many historic facades, which would otherwise have been lost, his insistence that post-war austerity should not be allowed to sacrifice all sense of line and suitability and the encouragement and need for integrity that he gave to his students, are all part of his memorial. He died at Ampthill on 3 February 1964, just before his eighty-fourth birthday. The results of two of his previous struggles still stand today and for both we should all be extremely grateful. In 1923 he read in the local paper that there were plans to pull down the attractive ruins of the historic Houghton House, which had already come to represent John Bunyan's House Beautiful. Few people could have withstood the apathy and opposition that he met with as he fought to save the house. It took just over seven years to get the money together but in December 1930, together with the Bedford Arts Club, he was able to buy the house, its site and access. Even then it took several more months of negotiations before the Office of Works took over responsibility for the ruined building and made it safe and weatherproof. Houghton House is an early 17th century building which was saved by the Professor. The cenotaph, made of Portland stone, which stands at the far end of the Alameda (Avenue) and the elaborate gates at the town end were designed by him, soon after his arrival in Ampthill. He had been asked to design war memorials in other towns and his plans had been gratefully accepted but at Ampthill his design was rejected. The rector described it as 'a pagan monument' and chose a simple gothic cross. The Professor refused to give up his design and after months of planning and fund raising he was able to design and install the tall obelisk which guides people's steps between the lime trees and carries their eyes on towards the distant horizon.

Ashby-St. Ledgers

THE GUNPOWDER PLOTTERS FLEE

In October/November of 1605, a story was passing up and down Watling Street, concerning some excellent horses that had been staged at the chief posting houses, such as those of St. Albans, Dunstable and Towcester; someone was preparing to make a very rapid journey. It was said that their owner was a Mr. Ambrose Rookwood, a wealthy young Roman Catholic gentleman who was a regular traveller along that road. His explanation was that he expected to join a hunting party at Dunsmore.

What actually happened on 5 November 1605 has become part of the folk history of this country. The discovery of the Gunpowder Plot and the story of the famous ride to safety by Rookwood and other conspirators started before sunrise on the morning of 5th November when Ambrose and Thomas Winter, his friend, learned that the Plot had been discovered and that Guy Fawkes had been arrested. They were only too aware that they must escape without drawing attention to themselves, so they set out to leave the city, and by 11.00 a.m. they were well into the countryside. Having decided it was safer to travel separately, they galloped along, taking advantage of the prepared relay of fast horses. Four other plotters had left ahead of them, (Catesby, Piercy, John and Christopher Wright) but Rookwood made such good time that he caught up with them at Little Brickhill, where he gave them the news of the failure of their scheme, and they all resumed their wild ride north. They pretended they were carrying Royal despatches to Northampton and raced through the various towns unchallenged, on their way to Ashby-St. Ledgers, and the safe haven of Catesby's house there.

Rookwood's dash from London (a distance of 80 miles) was completed in seven hours, the last thirty of these taking two hours, and undertaken on one horse.

Aspley Guise

THE FAMILY FROM GUISE

The descriptive Saxon name for this village described it as being in a woodland clearing near the aspen trees.

The Gyse family, who in the 13th century gave the village their name, came from an ancient Norman family.

ASPLEY GUISE (contd)

A HEALTH RESORT

In the mid 19th century, a Dr. Williams, who was a member of the Royal College of Surgeons, took up a medical practice in this rural area because he was suffering from a chest infection which he hoped would respond to the fresh wintry air.

He was delighted with the improvement to his health, and in 1856, published 'The Topography and Climate of Aspley Guise, In Reference to Health and Disease'. In this he discussed the benefits of the favourable climate and fresh country air as an aid to curing disease and strengthening of invalids. Many of his points, such as the advantages of pure water and the clear air found at higher altitudes, are still highly regarded today.

RICH BOYS AT THE CLASSICAL ACADEMY

As early as 1845, the Woburn historian, J. D. Parry, wrote in the Gentleman's Magazine that Aspley Guise was renowned for the number of genteel families who lived in the neighbourhood and that there were several private schools available for the children. The most famous of these was the Classical Academy. One old boy commented that next to Eton, Harrow and Rugby, it was the finest private school in England.

The most famous headmaster was probably William Wright; on a monument in St. Botolph's Church he is referred to as the second founder of the school. During Wright's time as headmaster there were about 140 boys and he offered them an all-round, Church of England based, education. In 1799 he built a gallery in the church where his boys could sit together.

By 1810 his successor, The Rev. Richard Pain, was offering: English, Latin, Greek, French, Writing, all sorts of Mathematics – including Merchants' accounts, Surveying and Navigation and Use of the Globes. His fees were 39 guineas (£40.95p) each year with Drawing, Dancing, Music and Military Exercises as optional extras. 1 guinea (£1.5p) was charged per quarter as a subscription to the Cold Bath and half a crown (12½p) per quarter as a subscription to the library.

There was a major outbreak of smallpox in 1824 which greatly harmed the school's reputation but from then on the headmasters prided themselves on the good wholesome food and medical attention provided.

POOR BOYS IN COURT
(A SHORT-SHARP-SHOCK!)

On the 22 January 1869, three 'lads', Luke Dickens, Fred Billington and Edward Cook, were charged with stealing apples from the orchard of an Aspley Guise Farmer. The apples were valued at just 2½p. and although the punishment of 3 months in prison for Dickens and 14 days for his two companions was not regarded as overstrict in the 19th century, it would certainly cause comment today!

Aynho

'GARDEN GLORY'

Ted Humphris, the well-known and acclaimed horticultural writer, author of 'Garden Glory', was born in Aynho, and was head gardener for many years at Aynho Park House. He received much praise for his orchids, pelargoniums and hippeastrums, and successfully exhibited at the Royal Horticultural Society's Shows. In his book 'Apricot Village' he explains how the village acquired its title.

APRICOT VILLAGE

Aynho, previously Aynhoe, which lies on the borders of Northamptonshire and Oxfordshire, was called 'Aienho' in the Domesday Book of 1086. This name, of Saxon origin, described a village founded by a family with a name such as Aega, which stood on a hill.

The name 'Apricot Village' goes back to feudal times when the villagers paid part of their rent to the Lord of the Manor in apricots! At that time, the gardens at Aynho Park House always had a 'reservoir' of young trees, grown specifically to replace old or damaged trees. Many of the houses today still have apricot trees growing up the front walls in espalier fashion, giving credibility to the old name.

THE VILLAGE TRAIL

During the school year 1979-80, the children of Aynho Church of England School produced a village trail, which was subsequently revised in 1986.

Starting in the Square they recorded that a weekly market had been held there on Tuesdays from 1324 until the late 17th century. Then the trail passes through the village, commenting on old features such as a replica of the village pump, the stocks and the apricot trees (see above). They offer a short or long trail, whichever the visitor prefers, and on each page they give helpful illustrations. What an interesting and useful way for children to study the history of their village.

Barton Seagrave

A FAMOUS ANTIQUARIAN

John Bridges who wrote the important 'History and Antiquities of Northamptonshire', which was published by T. Payne in 1791, was born here in 1666. He left the village to follow a legal career with the Customs and Excise but in his early fifties, he returned to Northamptonshire and began collecting material for his book.

He travelled to and fro across the county visiting as many towns and villages as possible and then, at his own expense, paid a team of local correspondents to copy out documents and the inscriptions on monuments and gravestones. He died in 1791, and was buried in St. Botolph's Church. It was his editor, Rev. Peter Whalley, who selected material from his enormous collection and published it in two volumes. His vast collection of manuscripts are now in The Bodleian Library, Oxford.

Battlesden

A SMALL COUNTRY ESTATE

As early as 1334, the landowner Thomas Fermbaud built a house at Battlesden and obtained a licence from the king to empark 200 acres of grass and woodland.

It changed hands several times and it was William Duncombe, before he died in 1603, who began to alter or even to rebuild the manor house. His son, Edward, inherited the estate and the family continued to live there for over 100 years. William had married Ellen Saunders, whose father had previously owned the adjoining estate of Potsgrove, as well as Battlesden Manor.

By the time that Gregory Page-Turner bought the estate in 1821, he felt that both the house and estate were in need of repair and modernisation. He, therefore, built an entirely new house nearer to the church, commissioned Sir Joseph Paxton (see Milton Bryan) to lay out new gardens and had two existing ponds turned into an ornamental lake. Unfortunately there is little left of this new house for us to see today because in 1885 the Page-Turner family sold it to the Duke of Bedford, who had most of it pulled down. Only the servants' quarters and stables were preserved for use as a shooting box.

BATTLESDEN (contd)
HE INTRODUCED THE SEDAN CHAIR

William Duncombe and Ellen (nee Saunders) had another son, whom they christened Saunders. This Saunders Duncombe travelled widely and is credited with introducing the sedan chair into England as a way of helping ladies to travel safely and cleanly through the London streets.

Bedford
F8

THE CASTLE AND ITS CONSTABLES

Alongside the northern bank of the River Ouse, at Bedford, is a large, grass-covered mound, which has been landscaped into the scenery. It is not far from Bedford Museum and the Cecil Higgins Art Gallery. This was once part of the foundations of Bedford Castle, a traditional stone building with an outer wall, moat and drawbridge. It must have been an impressive sight standing on the bank of what was then quite a wide and certainly very busy river. During the summer of 1224, this castle was so badly damaged that much of it was too dangerous to remain standing and the young King, Henry III, declared that it must never again be used as anything other than a private house.

A Saxon Fortress

The first reference to a 'fortress' at Bedford is in 918 when the monks, who put together the Anglo Saxon Chronicles, reported that: 'King Edward (of Wessex) went with his army to Bedford and occupied the fortress'; most of the garrison who had previously occupied it (the Danes) submitted to him. He remained there for four weeks, and before he left he ordered the fortress on the south bank of the river to be built. However, an entry for 1009 suggests that much of Bedford was burned during a Danish raid in that year.

Godric, the Saxon sheriff of Bedfordshire, who was probably in charge of whatever simple castle was left standing in Bedford, was killed during the Battle of Hastings.

The Normans Build a Castle

The victorious William Duke of Normandy, who was crowned King William I, divided England up among his family, friends and chief supporters. He made Ralph Tallebosc sheriff of Bedfordshire, and for his financial support and to strengthen his position in the county, gave him land, or complete villages, all over the county.

Although King William would have bitterly resented the nickname –

'Conqueror', he was well aware of the unrest in many Saxon towns and villages as the new Norman landowners took control. No actual fighting broke out in this county but it is probable that Ralph received orders to erect a stone-built castle on the banks of the River Ouse.

By the time that the clerks came round, in 1085, to assess land ownership in preparation for the great tax report of 1086, known as The Domesday Book, Ralph had died. His widow, Azelina, held Hockliffe and many other pieces of land, mainly in mid-Bedfordshire. They had no son, but their daughter, Matilda, appears to have married Hugh de Beauchamp. By 1086 he was sheriff and had the second largest holding of land in the county next only to the King. He owned forty scattered manors from Linslade in the west to Stotfold in the east, from Keysoe and Risely in the north to Streatley in the south. As was the custom, Hugh used many of the manors, especially those that were some distance from Bedford, to support his more important retainers, so that at anytime that it should be necessary he could call upon them for support.

The Beauchamp Family

Although the Beauchamp estates do not always pass directly from father to son, it was Miles de Beauchamp, grandson of Hugh, who was first to have need of these retainers to defend the castle.

The position of sheriff and the charge of Bedford Castle was the gift of the King, but with the permission of the King the large estates owned by Hugh de Beauchamp should have automatically passed to his heir. The Beauchamp family considered that the charge of the castle should also pass with their Barony. It appears that after Hugh's death, sometime early in the 12th century, his elder son, Simon, inherited his estates and was confirmed as constable of the castle. Also when Simon died, sometime before 1138, the estates passed to Miles, son of Simon's younger brother, Robert, and once again Stephen confirmed the straightforward transfer of the castle.

For the dispute and later Civil War, between King Stephen and his cousin Matilda, daughter of Henry I, see under Northampton, but in 1137 Stephen was in great need of loyal and powerful friends. Wishing both to help and to obligate the powerful Earl of Leicester, he arranged a marriage and income for the Earl's younger and landless brother. The young man known as Hugh le Poer (or Poor) was affianced to the even younger daughter of the dead Simon de Beauchamp, cousin of Simon's heir, Miles. King Stephen then notified Miles that he had created Hugh le Poer, Earl of Bedford, and that he wished Miles to surrender the castle to his cousin by marriage. Miles was greatly concerned; a request from a King like Stephen was very definitely an order and if he surrendered the castle, would he then be asked to give up the family

BEDFORD (Contd)

estates in Bedfordshire? Tentatively he agreed to the first if the second, i.e. the land, was guaranteed to be his by right of inheritance. Stephen asked him to surrender peacefully and he would recompense him in many other ways, but Miles felt that his position was strong enough to refuse.

The Castle Is Besieged

Opinions differ as to where Stephen spent the great court festival of Christmas 1137. Worthington Smith, the Dunstable antiquarian, suggests that he was at Kingsbury, his royal residence in that town. Sometime over the Christmas period, Stephen sent a final message to Miles and then marched his soldiers to Bedford and set up a siege. The contemporary writer, Henry of Huntingdon, complained that Stephen set the siege on Christmas Eve and completely ignored the holy season. Miles and his brother Payne resisted the siege, having stocked all the available store sheds with food and produce which his soldiers had taken by force from the townspeople of Bedford. Although Stephen had to take some soldiers away to settle another uprising, the main part of his army stayed in place, completely isolating the castle for five weeks. Battering rams and armaments failed to take the castle, but eventually the stores ran out. Just as Miles and his followers were near to starving, Stephen's brother, Henry Bishop of Winchester, arrived in Bedford, and persuaded them to surrender, and Hugh le Poer then became constable of the castle.

The Struggle Goes On

During 1137 Stephen was troubled by uprisings in Wales, Scottish raids over the borders of Northern England and the declaration by Earl Robert of Gloucester that he intended supporting his step-sister Matilda's claim to the throne. For the next few years Stephen had to diplomatically seek support and even at times fight for his throne. Then in early February 1141 there was a major battle at Lincoln; the fighting was long and hard and King Stephen was taken prisoner. Matilda was appointed Lady of England, and was able to reward her supporters. Hugh le Poer was forced to surrender Bedford Castle and Miles Beauchamp was once more in control, but not for long. He died shortly afterwards and until the next attack his brother Payne was in charge.

In 1146 Ralph, Earl of Chester changed sides and took his army to join up with Stephen who was once again crowned King of England. His soldiers broke through the defences of Bedford Castle, which was again held for the King.

The Future King Henry II

However, on or about 6 January 1153, Duke Henry, Matilda's son, landed in England to fight for the throne on his own behalf. (See under Northampton). He and his army marched from one of Stephen's strongholds to another, consistently winning people to his side. He did not stop to besiege Stephen's supporters who were sheltering in Bedford Castle but set fire to the town and continued on his way to Wallingford in Berkshire. Both Henry and Stephen were anxious to undertake a decisive battle but their senior advisers persuaded them that no good could come of a battle where 'Kinsman was pitted against Kinsman' and whoever won England would be left in great distress and bitterness. A truce was arranged. Both armies then proceeded towards Suffolk where many lives were lost and much property needlessly destroyed. On 17 August 1153 Stephen's son Eustace died, possibly from some sort of seizure or heart attack and to add bitterness to the situation, on the same day, Henry's first, legitimate son, William, was born. Up until November 1153 the two armies continued to move about the country but at long last a verbal and then written agreement was worked out. During his lifetime, Stephen should remain King of England, Duke Henry should be his heir.

Stephen died less than twelve months later, on 25 October 1154. The chroniclers described the cause as '. . . a chronic flux of haemorrhoids'. King Henry II was crowned in Westminster Abbey on 19 December 1154 and Bedford Castle was once more restored to Payne de Beauchamp. Responsibility for the castle stayed with the Beauchamp family, until some years later Payne's grandson had once again to fight for his inheritance.

King John and Magna Carta

King Henry II had brought peace to England and secured the position of the Beauchamps of Bedford. His youngest son, King John, ruled in such a domineering and overbearing way that England was once again at risk of civil war. Groups of church and secular leaders met at St. Albans Abbey to discuss what could be done and eventually it was decided to get John to sign a list of 'Articles' based on the ancient laws of the realm, ascribed traditionally to Edward the Confessor and included in the Coronation Charter of Henry I.

The de Beauchamp Family And Magna Carta

Payne de Beauchamp died c.1155 when his son, Simon, was still too young to inherit and the Sheriff of Bedfordshire administered his estates until c.1164. He was himself sheriff from 1194–1197. He died c.1206 and was succeeded by his son, William. As the Beauchamp family were in

BEDFORD (contd)

control of Bedford Castle, their support for Magna Carta was very important. If they gave a lead most of the other Bedfordshire landowners would follow.

In between the meeting at St. Albans Abbey on 4 August 1213 and the signing of Magna Carta, nearly two years later, there were numerous meetings, dispatches, appointments made – and broken – until, in desperation, the northern barons met at Stamford (Lincs.) where they were joined by William de Beauchamp of Bedford. Together they marched to Northampton where King John had promised to meet them. When he failed to appear they marched on to Bedford Castle and as there was still no message from the King marched on towards Windsor where he was staying and camped at Brackley (Berkshire).

King John refused to sign their charter so the barons raised a small army and laid siege to Northampton Castle. John's reply was to call for a truce and suggest a court of arbitration under a 'chairman' appointed by the Pope. The barons were tired of pointless discussion and broken promises so they marched on and successfully took London.

The Signing Of Magna Carta

Behind the scenes, the Archbishop of Canterbury and William, Earl Marshal of England, were going to and fro helping to shape the list of articles into a charter which would benefit all England. They persuaded the barons to return to Berkshire where they camped at Staines, chose a field by the Thames midway to Windsor (Runnymede) and arranged for them to meet the King. Intense discussions ended with the writing out of sixty-three 'Articles' on a piece of parchment 10½ inches by 21¾ inches headed 'These are the articles that the barons seek and the King concedes', and on or about 15 June 1215 John added his seal.

For a few months all went well but a letter from the Pope in September described the charter as 'unlawful' and 'unjust' and declared it 'null and void' because the seal had been obtained by force. Later in the month when the Archbishop went to Rome for the 4th Lateran Council he was arrested by the Pope for not giving John more support.

The Charter Is Ignored

The barons realised that the charter no longer held and armed themselves against the King. Soon, groups of soldiers were moving about the country and by the end of November, the mercenary, Falkes (Fawkes) de Breauté brought an army to Bedford and stormed the castle. William de Beauchamp escaped, but on 2 December the castle fell and Falkes was told to repair and strengthen it. His first local outrage was to take down the walls of St. Paul's church and St.

Cuthbert's church and use the stone for the castle. Then he rode to St. Albans and on 18 December met King John at the Abbey to discuss strategy; he then went on to defend London whilst John and his soldiers marched north to rally support.

Falkes De Breauté

King John employed numerous mercenary soldiers, but Falkes was a professional soldier who had settled in England and had become one of John's most trusted senior officers. In December 1215, he had taken Bedford Castle, in the name of the King; shortly afterwards he was put in charge of it and held it for the next nine years.

The struggle continued throughout 1216 until, during an October visit to Newark, at the age of forty-nine, John died quite suddenly from dysentery. Contemporary writers blamed his illness on a surfeit of peaches and new cider.

Henry III Is Crowned

His son Henry was only nine years old and the barons knew that England would be administered by the respected William Marshall. On 12 November 1216, a fortnight after Henry III's coronation at Gloucester, a slightly reworded charter was re-issued and most of the barons declared their loyalty to the new King. However, Falkes de Breauté was still in possession of William de Beauchamp's castle and estates; also Prince Louis of France, who had been welcomed by William, when he arrived to fight against King John in 1216, was still in the country with a large company of soldiers. Matters came to a head with a fierce battle in Lincoln during the summer of 1217 where Falkes captured William de Beauchamp and was rewarded by being made sheriff of Bedfordshire and Buckinghamshire. William submitted to the young King Henry, was pardoned and got back his land, though not the castle.

Falkes de Breauté Causes Trouble In Luton

William Marshall junior had inherited the manor of Luton during the troubled period leading up to the struggle for Magna Carta. He actively supported the barons and when his young wife died in 1216, King John gave his estates to Falkes de Breauté. Falkes had a castle built, between St. Mary's church and the River Lea; the river was diverted to make the moat and many people either lost their homes or had their ground floors flooded. His soldiers robbed the market stalls and householders and terrified not only the townspeople but all for many miles around.

And Elsewhere

While he was in charge of William de Beauchamp's estates he did great damage and sold off many of the livestock. When he needed to

BEDFORD (contd)

repair Bedford Castle, he not only took stone from St. Paul's church but also helped himself to timber from the woodland owned by Warden Abbey. In the struggle that followed a monk was killed and thirty other men, who tried to prevent the theft, were dragged through the mud and imprisoned in Bedford Castle. Maybe the soldiers were more violent than Falkes intended; at a later date he went to the abbey and did penance.

Nevertheless he and his soldiers visited St. Albans, sacked the town, entered the abbey through a back door, killed the cook and threatened to burn down both the town and abbey. The Abbot paid him with 100 lbs. of silver to leave them in peace. According to the chronicler at the abbey, some nights later he had a nightmare, woke his wife and described how he had seen an enormous stone falling from the abbey roof and crushing him to death. His wife recognised this as an omen and sent him back to St. Albans Abbey to do penance. The chronicler describes with glee how Falkes' bare back was whipped by each monk in turn. However, they also said that he had only done the penance to please his wife and that he refused to return the silver. Another cause for concern was that although the king's council had decided to restore Bedford Castle to William de Beauchamp, Falkes had refused to give it up.

Falkes de Breauté Is Charged In Court

Since 1211 or before Falkes had been a loyal and brave soldier in the service of both Kings and despite all the complaints Henry was slow to interfere. Some people feel that Falkes' behaviour was not barbaric in a 13th century context. Then in 1223 he was suspected of being involved in a conspiracy in Wales; he was certainly known to be friendly with the King's enemies. During Christmas 1223/24 he went to Northampton and surrendered his castles and royal honours.

The people of Luton had several times taken him to court but each time he failed to appear. When in July 1224 they took their grievances to the King's judges, meeting at Dunstable Priory, Falkes knew they would have to find him guilty. The three judges arrived and thirty-two people from Luton made their claims mainly of stolen land, e.g. Roger de Hoo accused Falkes of taking 30 acres from his father. Falkes was found guilty on all charges, heavily fined and it was recommended he should be outlawed.

Kidnap At Dunstable

Falkes was away when his brother William, and a group of soldiers, rode out from Bedford Castle to kidnap the judges! News reached

Dunstable in time for them to escape in different directions; two of them got away but Henry de Brayboc rode straight into a trap and was carried off to Bedford Castle. His wife, Christiana, and her escort rode to Northampton to beg the King for help, but this time Falkes had gone too far, and when summonded to attend the King he escaped to the estates of his friend the Earl of Chester on the Welsh border. Henry sent for Falkes, who had already ridden off to Bedford; when he realised that Falkes had slipped away he issued orders that Bedford Castle should be surrounded and began to plan for a major siege. Without waiting to finalise his plans he set off south with his church leaders, Chief Justice and the barons who were with him. No doubt William de Beauchamp was consulted about strategic points concerning the castle's defence although his presence is not recorded at Northampton. Henry was only sixteen years old but he had grown up with soldiers and sieges were to him a familiar form of warfare. He and his advisors made plans as they rode along and by the time that they stopped for the night at Newport Pagnell Henry was ready to send off messages in all directions. These 'messages' were royal commands and were to be obeyed 'in haste' or 'without delay'.

BEDFORD (contd)

The Siege Of Bedford Castle

A siege was a slow operation and Henry prepared for a long wait; a royal tent was to be sent from London and thirty casks of wine. The cooks might be able to use locally produced food supplemented with almonds, spice and ginger from the royal stillroom, but the wine which was to be provided from Northampton might not be good enough for use in the royal tent! Although he had sent for his sporting dogs, this was not going to be a country picnic where the attackers sat feasting until the castle starved; Brayboc and the other prisoners must be quickly released. The whole siege plan was prepared as they rode; many of the weapons were too big to transport, so their construction was allowed for on site. From Newport, messages were sent out ordering the local sheriffs to provide hides for making slings, and cords and cables to work the engines; the sheriff of London was to send wax to grease the cords, the monks at Newnham (near Bedford) were to provide 'raw-stone' to be made into shot, the sheriff of Bedfordshire was to send for quarry-men and masons (from Totternhoe?) to come with their tools to work the stone into shot. Smaller weapons could be transported, so at the Tower of London smiths were to work day and night making crossbows for immediate use and others were to be transported from distant Corfe Castle. The waxed cords and hides were used to make slings and to 'throw' large blocks of stone by using a winch. The account of the battle in the Dunstable Priory annals describes the use of mangonels. They had to be set up some distance from the castle and to the horror of the local people, the church leaders stood by and allowed the engineers to take down the towers of St. Paul's and St. Cuthbert's churches!

The letters went out from Newport on Thursday 20 June; at Bedford, on three successive days, a group of military and church leaders, including the Prior of Newnham, had demanded, in the King's name, the surrender of the castle. William de Breauté had defied them saying it was his brother's castle and that the King could not demand entry; when messengers told Henry this he swore to hang them all! The Archbishop of Canterbury arrived and on 20 June read the solemn service of excommunication on all who held the castle against the King. On 21 June the King arrived and the siege had officially begun. When, many weeks later, it was decided to make a major attack, 'the men of Dunstable', who had suffered attacks from Falkes and his soldiers and suffered the indignity of the kidnap, were allowed (a doubtful honour) to lead the attack. Their account is so clear that I now include part of a new translation by Mrs. Elizabeth North.

The Siege As Reported In The Annals of Dunstable Priory

'. . . the castle was captured in this way. On the east there was one petrary and two mangonels which attacked the tower every day. On the west side there were two mangonels which battered the old tower. And there was one mangonel on the south and one on the north which made two entrances in the walls nearest them. Besides these, there were two wooden towers made by a carpenter raised above the top of the tower and castle for the use of crossbowmen and spies. In addition to these there were several engines in which both crossbowmen and slingers hid in ambush. In addition there was a siege-engine called the Cat, beneath which underground diggers called miners could go in and out while they undermined the walls of the tower and castle. However, the castle was taken in four assaults. In the first the barbican was captured where four or five outsiders were killed. In the second the outer bailey was captured, where several were killed and our men acquired horses with harness, breastplates, crossbows, oxen, bacon and live pigs and count-less other plunder. However they burnt the outhouses with the corn and hay which were inside. In the third assault a wall near the old keep fell because of the action of miners and our men entered there and seized the inner bailey in face of great danger. In this occupation many of our men perished. Ten of our men, too, wishing to enter the keep, were shut in and held by the enemy. But at the fourth assault, on the Eve of Assumption, about the time of vespers, miners set fire to the keep so that smoke poured into the room in the keep where the enemy were; the keep cracked with the result that fissures appeared in its side. Then since the enemy despaired of their safety, Fawkes' wife and all the women with her, and Henry, the King's Justiciar, with the other knights who had previously been imprisoned, were allowed to leave safe and sound and the enemy subjected themselves to the King's commands, hoisting his standard at the top of the keep, thus they remained under royal guard in the keep that night. But the following morning, they were brought before the King's tribunal and absolved from excommunication by the bishops; more than eighty were hanged on the instructions of the King and justiciar.

After these events, Fawkes was taken to Bedford with a small escort. His men were absolved but he remained under pain of punishment until he should restore to the King the Castle of Plympton, the Castle of Stokes-Curci, gold and silver vessels, and the money which he had, thus he was brought to London.

Meanwhile a sheriff was ordered to destroy the keep and outer bailey, but the inner bailey remained for William Beauchamp to live in after the removal of the battlements and the filling in of the ditches on all sides. However, the stone was granted to the canons of Newnham and

BEDFORD (contd)

Cauldwell and the church of St. Paul at Bedford. Afterwards, Fawkes was absolved in London and because he had taken the cross he was allowed to leave for Rome'.

After The Siege

William de Beauchamp lived on for over thirty-five years. In 1234 he was appointed Baron of the Exchequer and Sheriff of Bedfordshire and Buckinghamshire in 1235 and 1236. He did not die until 1260 but in 1257, when he was at least seventy years old, he passed the Barony of Bedford to his second son, another William.

The Last Beauchamp of Bedford

This second William died within five years of receiving the title leaving a brother, John, who was too young to inherit and it was not until May 1265 that he legally received his inheritance. Three months later he was killed in the Battle of Evesham, fighting with Simon de Montfort, who was also killed. John was still a young man and this was his first battle. 'Who' said the chronicler at St. Albans Abbey 'could keep from tears at the death of John de Beauchamp'. The victory had been won by the skill of the young Prince Edward (later Edward I) and he was given the Beauchamp lands.

When John died there was still a niece of his living, Simon's daughter, Joan. When her father died in 1256 Henry III had placed her under the guardianship of William de Clare. The poor young lady was passed from one wealthy and influential person to another. Marriages were arranged for her and cancelled and she died unmarried c.1266.

Eventually, the Beauchamp land was divided between her female relatives. The site of the castle, still apparently in a derelict condition, passed to a distant relation and the distinguished name of Beauchamp was no longer connected with Bedford.

INNS AND INNKEEPERS

The Victorian Traveller's Guide to 19th Century England and Wales describes Biggleswade as 'a neat town on the Ivel, by means of which it carries on a considerable trade in timber, coals and oats'. This was in the early years of the 1860's when the population was only just over 4,000. Although the River Ivel was still providing work for some of the local families, many more were employed in the inns. As is increasingly common today, the Guide gave the prices for Bed and Breakfast separately. In a town the size of Biggleswade the former was likely to be 1s. 6d. to 2s. 6d. (12½p) and the latter 1s. 6d. to 2 shillings. The writer noted that gratuities or tips were a great problem, and commended those innkeepers who included them in the bill. He then guided travellers who were only stopping for a meal to pay the waiter at least 6d. (2½p). If a single gentleman stayed overnight he should tip the servants at least 1 shilling per day, or if he stayed with his wife and occupied both a bedroom and a sitting room he must expect to tip at least 2s. 6d. per day. Both innkeepers and their staff made a good living from the hundreds of travellers who stayed at the Biggleswade inns. Of the many which stood side by side along the main roads, the Victorian Guide recommended The Swan, The Rose and The Crown.

LANDLORD OF THE SUN INN

As early as 1668 John Brown, landlord of The Sun, was sufficiently well established to issue his own halfpenny-tokens. When the owner, George Fletcher, died in 1770 he had forty four horses in his stables with six post-chaises and two carriages, so he had obviously invested in the posting (or hiring) business.

At that time there were two kitchens equipped with both a large range and an open Dutch oven, stew pans, fish kettles and a bellows for blowing up the fire when guests arrived. To cater for his more genteel customers, Fletcher had coffee, chocolate and tea pots together with quantities of cups and saucers. Not only did his well-stocked cellars contain a great quanity of beer, port, madeira, claret and hock but he had also laid down quantities of brandy, cherry and raspberry brandy.

To give some idea of the number of high class guests he was prepared to house, in his linen cupboard there were eighty five pairs of sheets. Nearly a century later the landlord was still advertising superior stabling with double and single horse boxes and a lock-up coach house.

John Byng, Viscount Torrington, who is mentioned elsewhere in this

BIGGLESWADE (contd)

book, regularly stayed at The Sun c.1790. Byng only paid 10d. for his breakfast, 1 shilling (5p) for his dinner and 1s. 6d. for his supper but he paid 2s. 6d. (12½p) for his wine. Experienced traveller that he was he particularly admired The Sun and looked forward to the good food provided by Mistress Knight, the landlady.

Bletsoe   E5

SCRIMMAGE AT THE FALCON

On the 20 March 1869, David Jaquest went for a drink, at his local, the Falcon Inn. He was disturbed by the noisy behaviour of two tramps who were sitting across the room from his quiet corner. It was only 6.30 in the evening, but he decided that one of the men, (who turned out to be a travelling sawyer) called Thomas Harris, had had too much to drink. Rather foolishly, Jaquest accused Harris of this and told him and his wife, Sarah, to keep quiet. This was sufficient provocation to start the scrimmage. Sarah Harris slapped Jaquest's face and he tried to defend himself. Thomas Harris struck Jaquest in her defence and soon all three were fighting on the floor! At one stage, when Thomas Harris was on top of Jaquest, he thought he felt the lady's hands in his pockets. However, as his head was bleeding at the time, he omitted to check his pockets, concentrating on stemming the flow of blood. He went outside to wash and when he returned, both Thomas and Sarah Harris had gone.

He put his hands in his pockets and to his horror found them empty; he had lost 3 half crowns (each 12½p) and a florin (10p). He hurried after them and demanded his money, but they refused to halt or talk to him, so Jaquest fetched Superintendent Carruthers who arrested them at 'Whitbread's' public house at Sharnbrook, and, when they were searched the money was in their pockets as Jaquest suspected. They were taken to court, found guilty and both sentenced to 2 months hard labour.

THE BIBLE WINDOW

The church of St. Mary's contains an exceptionally fine, modern, stained glass window.

The four-hundredth anniversary of the Open Bible coincided with the death of Harry Cheetham, whose brother Alfred Cheetham had been the rector of St. Mary's from 1936 to 1945. Harry Cheetham was a printer who founded the Broadwater Press in Welwyn Garden City; he died 6 May 1938. It was, therefore, decided to erect a window which would not only commemorate the life of Harry Cheetham, but also the fact that four hundred years previously Thomas Cromwell had ordered that an English translation of the Bible should be placed in every parish church.

It was Mr. H. Warren Wilson who designed the window which includes St. Jerome and the Vulgate Bible which he translated into Latin at the end of the 4th century, John Wycliffe who in the 14th century began to translate the Bible into English, Gutenberg who invented printing in the 15th century and produced the first printed Bible and William Caxton who started the first English printing press in the second half of the century. Miles Coverdale also appears; in 1535 he produced the first complete English Bible. Many other men connected with different versions of the Bible are also represented, but it was Coverdale's which in 1538 was distributed around the churches.

Blunham K7

JOHN DONNE, POET AND PREACHER

The Earl of Kent, from Wrest Park, was patron of the living of St. Edmund's church and in 1614 he presented John Donne, Deane of St. Paul's, to the rectory of Blunham. Unlike some 17th century rectors, it is said that he regularly visited his rural parish and was able to communicate with the people of two such different communities. Some of his sermons, edited by G. R. Potter and E. M. Simpson, have been published and his poems can be found in several different anthologies. Because of the internationally famous film, based on the book, by Ernest Hemingway, 'For Whom the Bell Tolls', thousands of people who are quite unaware of the Rev. John Donne and his other poems, will quote today:-

'No man is an Island . . .'
or
'. . . never send to know for whom the bell tolls; it tolls for thee'.

At the age of 27 he married a 16 year old girl called Anne. Despite their comparitive prosperity their shared experience was typical of 17th century life. Out of 12 children they only managed to rear six. When his wife died in childbirth at the age of 32, five children had already died.

The Oxford Book of Seventeenth Century Verse (Clarendon Press 1934) contains two sad epitaphs both published in 1616, two years after he took up his position at Blunham.

BLUNHAM (contd)

'On My First Daughter'
'Here lies to each her parents' ruth,
Mary, the daughter of their youth:
Yet, all heaven's gifts, being heaven's due,
It makes the father less to rue.
At sixe months end she parted hence,
With safety of her innocence;'

'On His First Sonne'
'Farewell, thou child of my right hand, and joy;
My sinne was too much hope of thee, lov'd boy,
Seven yeeres thou' wert lent to me, and I thee pay,
Exacted by thy fate, on the just day.'

Boughton G12

'CAPTAIN SLASH' AND HIS GHOST

The famous medieval fair, which was held in this village on 24-25-26 June every year until 1916, tended to attract troublemakers and petty thieves, as do other entertainments of this type.

The most notorious of these was George Catherall, nicknamed 'Captain Slash'. He and his band had for some time terrorised the neighbourhood, and, after the fair of June 1826, they lay in wait for traders and visitors leaving the fair. Catherall was caught, taken to Northampton, tried, and eventually hanged on 21 July 1826. There is a legend that, to defy his mother, who had always said that he would die with his boots on, he kicked them off before mounting the scaffold!

Within sight of the fairground are the ruins of St. John the Baptist's church. These attractive ruins have the reputation of being haunted and the most persistent ghost is said to be the notorious 'Captain Slash'.

Brackley D18

THE SANCTUARY – BREAKERS' PUNISHMENT

The ancient right of sanctuary is still from time to time a point of discussion, especially the rights and wrongs of the breaking of sanctuary by the authorities.

There can seldom have been a more bizarre punishment given to offenders than that meted out to some Brackley men who dragged a suspected criminal out of sanctuary in the year 1200. Without waiting for the authorities, they took the law into their own hands and hanged the accused without trial. First the offenders were stripped of all their clothes, except their underpants, then they were forced to dig up the decaying corpse from where they had buried it, at the foot of the makeshift gallows, and finally, they had to carry it on their shoulders for nearly a mile to Brackley church.

On arrival there, they had to carry the decaying body shoulder high around the church, while they were 'solemnly scourged' (whipped on their back and shoulders with pointed, metal barbs). After the body had received Christian burial, the offenders had to walk barefoot from Brackley all the way to Lincoln, process around the cathedral city and be scourged outside each and every church there.

THE MAN WHO INVENTED 'CATALOGUES'

Thomas Payne, who was born here in 1717, grew up in this town and then travelled to London to work with his brother Oliver who lived in The Strand.

BRACKLEY (contd)

Although their main work was selling books, they are remembered for their innovative work, producing catalogues. This was still a very new idea; they listed books under subject, quality and binding. Payne's wide ranging catalogue, published on 29 February 1740, is regarded as one of the first of its kind. The success of this volume encourged Thomas to continue and from 1755 until he handed the business over to his son in 1790, he produced one or more volumes each year.

He married a lady called Elizabeth Tayler and they took over her father's shop, which, because of the many famous writers who were their frequent visitors, became London's first literary Coffee House.

Brigstock K6

QUEEN PHILLIPPA'S DEER PARK

This village was once surrounded by the trees of Rockingham Forest. It was Edward III, who agreed that his Queen, Phillippa, could enclose an area to make a deer park. He employed Walter de Wyght to mark out the enclosure with a boundary made from a fence of palings, set on a high bank, beside a ditch. Wyght was to build two lodge gates and to improve the parkland by cutting down any unwanted trees. Timber was of course, valuable and Wyght's instructions were to account for the trees which were cut down and to be sure and find out which method would be most profitable, to sell them, or to retain them for charcoal production on the royal estate.

WILLIAM PARR

The position of 'Keeper' in the 16th century was one of overall responsibility for the running of the park and William Parr, who was 'Keeper of the Park' in the 1520's, was a wealthy man, and at one time became sheriff of the county. He was related by marriage to Catherine Parr, the sixth wife of Henry VIII. He was responsible for building the first stages of the manor house.

FILM STARS VISIT BRIGSTOCK

Four hundred years later, Herbert Wilcox, film director and husband of the famous film star, Anna Neagle, bought the manor house and during the years leading up to the war many of their theatre friends used the house for weekends out of London.

Campton   J12

THE SPEAKING WALL

Both Bedfordshire and Northamptonshire are fortunate to have not
only several major historic houses, but also numerous surviving smaller,
but equally interesting, manor houses.

History teachers today are anxious to help children understand what
life was really like for the people who once lived in our villages and
towns. It is easy to say, 'If only walls could talk' but how wonderful if
they really could! There is nothing at Campton to tell us that a 16th
century owner, Thomas Palmer, was executed in 1553 for supporting the
coronation of the young Lady Jane Grey. However, on a wall, in the
'new' manor house, built by the Ventris family after Palmer's death, is a
plaque which was put up by Sir Charles Ventris, to commemorate a
lucky escape, in 1645.

He was a Royalist officer at a time when Bedfordshire was controlled
by Parliament. Desperately short of money, he came home in 1645 to
try and collect his rents but was surprised by a party of Parliamentary
soldiers. It is said that he was asleep, when they first arrived, and just
had time to pull on his uniform and rush downstairs, before they forced
their way into the house. As he dived for the window a soldier fired
point blank, and missed! The bullet was embedded in the panelling.

Sir Charles escaped and returned to his regiment but when he finally
returned home, at the end of the war, he ordered that the bullet hole
should be carefully preserved and a plaque be put up to record his
miraculous escape. Both are there to this day, although the house is not
open to the public.

Cardington   H9

THE MAN WHO WORKED FOR PRISON REFORM

John Howard, the man who is rightly famous for his work on prison
reform, was born in 1726. His father, who was a reasonably well-to-do
upholsterer, had his private house at Hackney and his business at Long
Lane, Smithfield. John was not a healthy boy and his young life became
even more restricted by the death of his mother when he was only five.
His father arranged an apprenticeship for him with a firm of wholesale
grocers but he was far from happy and when his father died John
cancelled his indentures. Being still only sixteen, and having inherited a
reasonable sized fortune, he had plenty of time to gain more experience

of life before he settled down. For five or six years he travelled in France and Italy then spent some years living quietly in England. During this period he married the lady in whose house he was lodging, but she died two years later.

The event which was to change his life occurred in 1756, the year that, under George II, England and France eventually started to fight in an attempt to settle their borders in North America. Howard set sail for a visit to Portugal but his ship was captured by a French privateer. The six days that he spent in a prison at Brest and the unpleasant treatment that he received during the next few weeks, before being exchanged with a French army officer, made him acutely aware of the horrors of life in prison.

On returning to England he married a distant relation, Henrietta Leeds, and as she also had poor health they tried to find an estate in the country. In 1762, they moved into a comfortable house, which Howard had inherited, in Cardington. His cousin, Samuel Whitbread, of Southill Park, was involved in the movement which was trying to improve life for the poor people of England.

One of Howard's first interests in rural life was in buying up and improving farm cottages, or in having them entirely rebuilt in brick and tile. He paid for the children of his tenants to learn to read, for the girls to learn sewing and the boys to learn writing and arithmetic. Most unusually for that period, although he and his family attended The Bunyan Meeting House in Bedford, he allowed his tenants and those families that he helped, to attend the church of their choice.

Three years after their arrival at Cardington, Henrietta was expecting their first child; their son John was born on 27 March 1765 but Henrietta died a few days later. Although Howard continued to live in the village and to take an interest in the local people, he was a very lonely man.

Soon afterwards, he became High Sheriff of Bedfordshire, and as he had to attend the assize courts he was brought face to face with men brought into court from the prison. He decided to visit Bedford prison and was shocked with what he saw; he visited prisons in other counties and found that their prisons were more likely to be worse than better.

His main concern was that gaolers were entirely unpaid; they relied for their income on fees that were paid by the prisoners, before they could leave prison. He was invited to present the evidence which he had collected to a Select Committee of The House of Commons and as a direct result of this meeting, two Bills were passed in 1774. One ordered that money should be taken from the rates to provide a salary for the gaoler and that men who were in prison for not paying the gaoler's fees should be released. The other ordered that checks should be made on the prisoners' health and, where necessary, medication should be provided.

Howard continued to visit prisons, travelling all over this country and then to and fro across Europe. The results of these travels, all paid for by himself, was the book, 'The State of the Prisons', which he published in 1777. This contained reports of the many prisons he had visited, discussion about the need for clean accommodation with separate infirmaries, workshops and chapels, and a great deal of advice about the type and quality of personnel who should be employed to work in the prisons.

He continued to travel; ignoring his own poor health he rode around England, sometimes travelling 40 miles in a day. When he landed on foreign soil he would travel hundreds of miles in a chaise, if necessary sleeping as they bumped along the rough roads. He was a strict vegetarian and had sensible ideas about health and hygiene in advance of the general view of his day.

Having experienced a solitary childhood himself he saw nothing wrong in sending his own motherless son away to school when he was only four years old. John junior was sent from school to school and then to college; not only his physical but his emotional health suffered. It is possible that he suffered brain damage at birth, which would have made school life particularly difficult. He became increasingly depressed and at 21 was unable any longer to care for himself and was put into an asylum. This was a terrible shock to his father and caused him great distress, even threatened to engulf him in hopeless despair. There was nothing that he could do to help his son, so in 1789 he set out once more, this time crossing to Eastern Europe. He became ill while he was visiting Kherson in the Ukraine and died on 20 January 1790.

He was buried in Russia and on his tomb is engraved:- 'Whosoever thou art, thou standest at the grave of thy friend'.

In 1866 the Howard Association was formed and in 1921 it became the Howard League for Penal Reform.

A PUBLIC SPIRITED LANDLORD

When Arthur Young rode into Bedfordshire in 1771, he had a most uncomfortable ride. He recorded that the road was 'a cursed string of hills and holes' with a 'causeway here and there thrown up, but so high, and at the same time so very narrow, that it was at the peril of our necks that we passed a waggon with a civil and careful driver'. He described these causeways as 'a pernicious and vile practice, which might be expected if thrown up at the expense of the farmers alone; but when found in a turnpike, deserves every unworthy epithet which frightened women and dislocated bones can possibly give rise to'!

But when he left Bedford and took the road to Northill, he was astonished to find, after he left the Biggleswade turnpike, that the road continued with a very fine causeway, of a good breadth and height, and

very level and free from ruts. He could scarce believe himself upon a
bye road which induced him to enquire who was responsible. He was
told that it was the 'excellent effect' of several gentlemen, particularly
John Howard Esq. of Cardington, who not only greatly assisted the
parish in making a fine causeway through the village, but himself
expended above £50 in making such a good road.

HOME OF
'THE WHITE KNIGHT'

A family from Lorraine had already settled here before the Norman Conquest; from being known as 'of Lorraine' the family name became 'Loring'.

The last male member of the family to live at Chalgrave was a famous soldier, Sir Nigel Loring. He fought successfully at the naval battle of Sluys and at Poitiers. He was a friend of Edward III's son, who was known as 'The Black Prince', and so he became one of the original Knights of the Garter. His arms can be seen at St. George's Chapel Windsor. He is said to be the soldier on which Conan Doyle based his story, The White Company.

When Sir Nigel died in 1386 he left his other manor, Sharnbrook, to his elder daughter, and the manor at Chalgrave to his younger daughter, Margaret, who was married to Thomas Pever, Lord of the Manor of nearby Toddington. A stone representation of Sir Nigel can be seen lying on his tomb in All Saints Church.

Chicksands

J11

HAPPINESS IN THE SUN

By the time that the Civil War (17th Century) drew to an end, Dorothy, daughter of a famous Royalist officer, Henry Osborne, of Chicksands Priory, knew that she wanted to marry William, son of an equally famous Parliamentarian, William Temple (Senior). Their marriage was forbidden, first by her father and then by her brother, but they continued writing to each other until they were eventually married, seven years later. Although the Osborne family had lost much of their wealth during the war, Dorothy was still able to live a comfortable life in the country house which her ancestors had adapted from the old priory buildings. Dorothy's home, still known as Chicksands Priory, is open to the public twice a month in the summer, on Sunday afternoons.

In the last year before they got married, William began to get very impatient and Dorothy was more and more distressed. One day she went for a walk across the common land near her home, and stopped to talk to the young girls in charge of the grazing cattle. That evening, in her letter to William, she explained that if only they realised it, these penniless but carefree girls, working outdoors in the summer sunshine, were amongst the happiest people in the world.

Clifton

RESCUE BY P.C. CURTIS

It appears that early in July 1896 a young lady tried to commit suicide by running into the river. She was seen by P.C. Curtis who without hesitation plunged into the water, fully dressed, caught the woman's clothes and brought her head to the surface. However, at that moment, James Ragan also sprang in and fell on top of the P.C. and the floundering girl, the result being that all three plummetted into very deep water. The constable (who in fact, was a non-swimmer) was in great danger of losing his life, but thankfully, managed to grasp some weeds, and from this precarious position he pulled Ragan to his feet. Just as the girl was going under for the third time, he caught hold of her dress and pulled her onto the bank. Meanwhile, Ragan had collapsed, but Curtis managed to haul him, unconscious, onto the bank, where he gave him artificial respiration until he regained consciousness. P.C. Curtis was later recommended for a gallantry award for his heroic actions.

Clipston

A DEDICATED BAPTIST FAMILY

During the 18th century, those families who preferred to worship God in independent chapels, rather than within the parish church, were still the subject of gossip and suspicion.

Robert Ellis had for many years been clerk of All Saint's Church in the village and as part of his duties he had to announce the psalms, using the introduction 'Let us sing to the praise and glory of God'. This bothered him because he quite often felt that the chosen psalms neither praised nor glorified.

He had heard that at nearby Faxton a group of men and women met every Sunday morning to worship God but without using the Book of Common Prayer or sticking to the strictly laid down form of service used by the Established Church.

One Sunday morning he screwed up his courage and rode over to Faxton. There was a warm welcome for him and an enjoyable service, so the next Sunday morning he asked his horrified wife to accompany him. She had not been all that pleased the previous Sunday when her husband deserted the parish church, and may have made excuses to cover up for his absence; certainly she had no intention of letting any of

CLIPSTON (contd)

the neighbours see her riding over to Faxton. She refused point blank. Her husband had feared that she would refuse, but he was so anxious for her to share his joy in this new form of worship, that he asked her once more to accompany him, and then called for two of his farm workers to come into the room, lift up his furious wife and place her onto the back of his own horse. Then he told them to take a rope and tie the two of them together!

So the poor woman rode all the way from Clipston to Faxton tightly tied behind her husband. The more fuss and noise she made the more she would call attention to their progress. Nevertheless the poor lady cried all the way, and on arrival suffered the indignity of being cut free and lifted down from the horse. However, despite this shameful introduction, she was won over by the sincerity of the local preacher and agreed to return the following Sunday. Before long both she and her husband were enthusiastic members of this new congregation.

Robert Ellis lived on, a happy and healthy man, until his 95th year, when one day, while kneeling at family worship, he fell forward and died. By this time the family were living at Bugbrooke but before leaving Clipston he had been one of the founder members of Clipston Baptist Church.

A DEVOTED MINISTER AND HIS CONGREGATION

A career as church minister is quite often a calling which people take up after some years of work experience following a totally different career. However, it must be unusual for a young man to work as hard as John Mack was obliged to do before he was eventually ordained. That he was a particularly gifted minister can be seen from the story below.

The Rev. John Mack was a poor boy born in Glasgow during 1788 and grew up to become first a weaver and then a soldier. He neglected his former job to read every book he could lay hands on, and while carrying out the latter position, he discovered that he had a natural gift as a preacher. Encouraged by his friends and advisers he tried to buy his way out of the army, but his commanding officer demanded either £100 or two Scottish soldiers to replace him. While his friends were raising the £100, Mack was appointed schoolmaster to his regiment; so successful was he in this new position, that when the £100 was eventually offered, the officer demanded two Scottish soldiers in addition to the money! Eventually Mack was free to travel to Bristol Academy and to enrol as a student minister.

In December 1812, while he was still a student, he visited Clipston Baptist Church, which at that time was without a minister. He returned during the long summer vacation of 1813 and was so popular with the congregation, that they aked him to stay on. He was extremely happy in Clipston and was sure that God wanted him to work there, but after all his struggles he was determined to complete his training and begged to be allowed to return to Bristol for his final year.

They agreed to this and so Mack continued to spend term time at the Academy and vacations at Clipston. During a visit in 1814, he baptised Anne Ellis who was the granddaughter of Robert Ellis (above) who had founded the church. They became close friends and immediately after ordination, when he took up the full time living at Clipston he and Anne were married and settled down to raise their family in the village.

Unfortunately Mack's health became an increasing problem and he died on 5 November 1831. He was only 42 and his young widow was left to support six children all under 12 years of age. In the years before state support for such children, this could have caused the break up of the family, but Mack and his wife had generated so much love and respect, both in Clipston and for some miles round about, that a sum of £1800 was collected for the family's support. An enormous sum of money in 1831, which enabled her to bring the family up within the security of a loving home and within the form of Christian faith which their great-grandfather had chosen.

John's death left Anne to bring up four sons and two daughters, single handed. James went to America, John to India, where he became

CLIPSTON (contd)

Deputy Harbour Master at Rangoon and then Superintendent of the Mercantile Marine Office and many other posts. He also became Deacon in the Baptist Church of Rangoon.

Robert, who was only 2 when his father died, sailed off to the East Indies when he was 13 years old. He was extremely happy out there but having saved enough in 9 years to take time off for a long stay back home with his mother, allowed her to persuade him to stay in this country. He became a well-known businessman in Newcastle and was a highly respected member of the Baptist Church in that city. In memory of his 'happy' childhood, he named his home 'Clipston House'.

William remained in this country and became first a bookseller and stationer in Bristol and then a London publisher. He is remembered as the man who originally published 'The Birthday Scripture Text Book' of which over 1 million copies were sold in his lifetime. He was active in the Bristol Baptist Church and for 17 years treasurer of the Bristol City Mission. One of his sons, Robert, published a popular serial publication, 'The Bristol Christian Leader'.

Robert Ellis's great-granddaughter, Mary and her husband carried the Baptist message with them to Burma and even in this country, there were still members of this amazing Baptist family who were prepared to carry their faith out from Newcastle to India. John's eldest son came back to join the several members of the family now settled in Newcastle, but when he married one of his cousins, they decided that they too should settle in Rangoon.

Little did Robert Ellis know on that fateful Sunday, back in the 18th century, when he obliged his employees to tie his wife up on the back of his horse and carried her crying with shame and embarrassment all the way to Faxton, that well over a century later, two of his great-great-grandchildren would marry and look forward to baptising their children, not as far away as Faxton or Bugbrooke, but on the other side of the world.

Clophill

DID DICK TURPIN VISIT CLOPHILL?

Dick Turpin is probably the best known highwayman who ever worked the roads of England. His main haunts were more likely to be along the Great North Road, but in all the counties north of London there are inns which claim to have been used by him for his various adventures. The Flying Horse, standing on the crossroads, in what, even today, is still quite an isolated position, is just the kind of place where robbers would have planned their attacks on innocent travellers, but whether Dick Turpin, as legend suggests, ever used this inn is hard to say.

Cockayne Hatley

THE VILLAGE NAME

The descriptive, Saxon name which became 'Hatley' was made up of a man's name, perhaps 'Haetta' and 'leah' meaning 'clearing in the wood'. The 'Cockayne' prefix came from the family of that name who came to the area in the 15th century. The father Henry Cockayne, who was Member of Parliament in 1421, had married into the powerful Grey family of Wrest Park.

MARGARET HENLEY: WENDY DARLING

The poet, W. E. Henley, who wrote these lines from 'Invictus':-

> "It matters not how strait the gate,
> How charged with punishments the scroll,
> I am the master of my fate
> I am the captain of my soul"

lived in the village and was buried in the churchyard of St. John's Church just outside the village itself. He was a great friend of J. M. Barrie and it is thought that Henley's daughter, Margaret, was Barrie's model when he was planning the young heroine who would befriend Peter Pan.

39

Collingtree
H14

AN UNUSUAL NAME FOR AN INN

In the middle of the attractive village of Collingtree is an old, thatched, public house called 'The Wooden Walls of Old England'. The descriptive Saxon name of this village was 'Cola's' Tree and the village was once part of Salcey Forest from where the timber is said to have been cut for Francis Drake's ship. Hence the name of this old inn.

Colmworth
J5

AN EARLY 15TH CENTURY WILL

Roger Benetheton, who was a chaplain connected with St. Denys' Church, made his will on 27 February 1439. Having bequeathed his soul to God, The Blessed Mary, and All Saints, and requested that he should be buried in the church cemetery, next to his father, he then set out to arrange his funeral.

The Rector was to receive 20 pence; 12 pence went to another clergyman, 4 pence to every clergyman who attended his funeral mass, with an extra 2 pence for those who stayed on for his burial. The Prior of Bushmead was to receive 2 shillings and any of the Bushmead canons who could get permission to attend were to receive 1 shilling; any of the local men who attended the funeral were to receive 1 penny. He provided 1 shilling for the hire of the bier (frame for carrying the coffin), 1 shilling for the hire of two palls to drape it with, 3 lbs. of wax to make candles to stand around the bier, 1 shilling for the torches (lights), 3 shillings to provide oil for the Sepulchre Light, not just for the period of the funeral, but also for the days which followed (to represent a chain of prayer), and finally 6 pence to the man who carried the holy water.

He was obviously quite a wealthy man because he was able to bequeath land and houses in Higham Ferrers (N) to Richard Butcher of Rushden (N). One shilling each to another six friends or members of his family, and 8 pence each to every inhabitant of Colmworth.

Then he began a long list of bequests to various charities. The houses of Friars were always poor; they owned little or no property and they were much respected for their unwordly and prayerful lives. Benetheton left 10 shillings to the Friars of Bedford and 10 shillings to the Carmelite Friars of Cambridge. Money which was collected at his funeral was to go to the churchwardens for the upkeep of St. Denys' Church, Colmworth, and 6 shillings and 8 pence for the upkeep of the church at Higham

Ferrers – (a John Benetheton had been vicar there earlier in the century).

During the 15th century there was no organised collection for the repair of roads and bridges, so he left 3 shillings and 4 pence for the upkeep of Bedford bridge and the same amount to help build a new bridge at St. Neots.

Last, but by no means least, is a bequest of 1 shilling to every maid (unmarried girl) in Colmworth 'fit for wedlock'. Even poor girls were expected to provide a dowry when they married, and for poor families with several daughters this could be a serious problem. The gift of a shilling could have made the difference between marriage or remaining at home, working as unpaid labour.

Cople   H8

HISTORIC BRASSES

In All Saints Church is an extremely old brass commemorating the life of Nichol Roland, a barrister who died in 1400, and another commemorating the life of Walter Roland who is portrayed in full armour, such as he would have worn at the Battle of Agincourt in 1415. This is probably the oldest military brass in Bedfordshire. Yet another 15th century brass in All Saints is a very attractive portrayal of another Cople landowner, John Launcelyn and his wife Margaret (née Roland). John died in 1435 and his property was divided between his two daughters. Cople was part of the inheritance of Anne who married Walter Luke. On their tomb is a brass which records her death in 1538 and his in 1544. Many of the Launcelyn family held important military and civil positions. Anne was nurse to the young Henry VIII; Walter Luke was knighted and became a judge of the King's Bench.

41

COPLE (contd)

The Luke Family Of Wood End, Cople

Nicholas, son of Walter and Anne, was a Commissioner for the Peace during the reign of Queen Elizabeth and became High Sheriff of Bedfordshire. His grandson, Nicholas (2) married Margaret St. John from the ruling Bedfordshire family. Although both Nicholas and Margaret died long before the Civil War, their son and grandson worked with their St. John relatives to support Parliament.

Sir Oliver Luke

Sir Oliver Luke was a respected Bedfordshire landowner. He was a supporter of the Puritans who wanted to raise the standards of the Established Church and regularly represented either Bedford Borough or the county in Parliament. In the years leading up to the Civil War, he was a militant leader amongst the group who were working for the freedom of Parliament. It was Sir Oliver Luke, who on 17 June 1642 was ordered to arrest Sir Lewis Dyve of Bromham. In 1643 the family raised a regiment of dragoons but Sir Oliver, who had been wounded at Bromham, took no further part in the fighting, giving his support from Parliament and helping to raise money, food and supplies.

Sir Samuel Luke

At the so-called Long Parliament, which started in 1640, Sir Oliver Luke represented Bedfordshire and his son, Sir Samuel, represented Bedford. However, at the opening Battle of Edgehill, in October 1642, he commanded a troop of horse which were dreadfully cut about by the Royalist attack. It was in the following year that he had his own regiment of dragoons and he took an active part in the Battle of Newbury where again he was in the centre of the fighting. A month later, the Royalist soldiers were driven out of the garrison at Newport Pagnell and by the end of the year, as Colonel Sir Samuel Luke, he became Governor. He remained there for the next eighteen months and when he left Newport Pagnell, after the successful Battle of Naseby, he returned to Cople and followed the quiet and peaceful pastimes of gardening and estate management.

Corby J6

A NEW TOWN – 1875

During the years 1875–1879 a particularly difficult piece of railway line was constructed between Kettering and Manton. It was only fifteen miles long but involved such complicated and labour intensive work that

2,500 temporary workers were employed. Navvies dug away the steeply sloping ground and miners bored a tunnel through the hills. By the time that they had finished Corby tunnel was nearly 2,000 yards long. The presence of these labour camps around the country has been well recorded, but few details were known about the way the occupants actually lived. The Rev. D. W. Barrett, of Nassington, made copious notes and sometime before 1880 he produced a book, 'Life and Work Among The Navvies'. He recorded that accommodation was found for some of the families in nearby villages, but that, in addition, camps were set up along the line including one made up of fifty wooden huts at Corby.

The Rev. Barrett also found that the workers were recruited from all over the country and that they were allowed to bring their wives and families with them. Each wooden hut had three rooms, a living room and two bedrooms. Many of the families slept together in one room, and let out the other bedroom to lodgers. Some of the huts were designated as 'shanties', i.e. huts which were licensed to sell beer.

At a time when the nearby agricultural workers were earning well under £1 per week, these unskilled navvies were earning from £1 to £1.55 and the skilled men up to twice as much. With beer at 3d. (1¼p) per pint, the hard working men consumed a frightening quantity. Some men lodged at the shanties and were charged 4d. a night for a bed, in a shared room, 1d. if they slept on the table and ½d. if they dossed down on the floor. The Rev. Barrett was impressed with the great sense of comradeship there was between the men.

He had an excellent opportunity of getting to know them and their wives and children. Although the men often had to work seven days a week, the Rector of Corby was allowed to organise a mission at the camps, and for a time the Rev. Barrett acted as chaplain.

Cranfield C10

THE CARRIER OF CRANFIELD

Throughout history, heavy wagons, farm carts and strings of pack-ponies have plodded up and down the roads of England, carrying goods and merchandise from the place of production to the town where they would eventually be processed or sold.

Probably the best known and most loved of these horse-drawn vehicles belonged to the local carriers. Every town, and most of the larger villages had one who followed regular routes, linking the people of their home village or town with London and other larger towns. Many of these businesses passed from father to son and were well-known all along their routes, where people would be waiting for them to pass by, and hoping they would sell a brace of rabbit or buy a new darning needle in exchange for a small sum of money.

Within living memory, a few of these carriers worked with horses and carts around the towns of the two counties. One of the best-known of these was Alf White, who ran his business from Cranfield. Although he replaced his 2-wheel horse-drawn cart with a Model 'T' Ford van in the 1920's, old habits die hard, and on stopping the van he could be heard to shout 'Whoa' at the inanimate 'horse'. Unfortunately, the coming of the double-decker open-top motor bus service to Bedford cut short his trading activities in the early 1930's.

Daventry C13

TRAVELLERS

Situated on the A45, which was once part of the Holyhead coaching road, Daventry has always been a centre for travellers. At one time eighty horse drawn coaches passed through the town each day. The town was and still is a central point where roads converge and busy people meet, hold conferences or carry out their business deals before moving on to another part of the country. In the years around 1825 travellers could leave London at 6.30 a.m. on the express 'Wonder' coach and with a twenty minute breakfast stop at Redbourne (near St. Albans) and a short lunch break at Northampton they could be at Daventry by 2.15 p.m.

Horses and horse drawn vehicles tore the road surfaces to pieces and during the years of the Civil War, long before the Turnpike Trusts made it possible to collect money for the repair of roads, the surfaces were indescribably rough.

THE CIVIL WAR

Apart from the Battle of Naseby, Northamptonshire does not often appear in books which cover the events of the Civil War. However, if one looks into the letter-books of the Royalist leader, Sir Lewis Dyve[1] of Bromham and of the Parliamentary leader, Sir Samuel Luke[2] (see Cople) one can see that not only was Daventry a central point which both sides used as a camping site as they moved about the country but also how badly the people suffered as a result of these visits.

The opening battle of the Civil War, at Edgehill on 23 October 1642, was far enough away that it was only the unnamed soldiers from Daventry who suffered. The soldiers who returned home through the town, during the days that followed the battle, were too new to war to ill-treat the townspeople or their property. By the time of the first Battle of Newbury, which took place eleven months later, money and supplies were short, officers were hardened and many of the soldiers were bitter and unpaid.

Sir Lewis Dyve took a detachment of Royalist soldiers to settle in for the winter at Newport Pagnell while his officers, with small groups of men rode to and fro across the Bedfordshire/Northamptonshire borders recruiting or pressing men and commandeering horses, carts and supplies. On 14 October another detachment of Royalist soldiers marched into Daventry pausing there long enough to gather what men and supplies they could. At that time neither side wished to alienate the people of Northamptonshire who had not come out strongly on behalf of either side. Nevertheless the Parliamentary officer, Colonel Fiennes, quartered his regiment near the town on the way home and the Royalist, Sir Richard Byron, did the same on 2 December followed by the King's nephew, Prince Maurice, four days later.

The Northamptonshire Committee wrote urgently to Sir Samuel Luke at Newport Pagnell, reporting that seven of their soldiers had clashed with a small group of Royalists and had taken four prisoners. They begged for help to get Prince Maurice and his foot soldiers away from Daventry, reminding Luke that Parliament relied on the local people there for supplying their own foot soldiers. Sir Lewis Dyve had been forced out of Newport Pagnell which was now in the hands of Sir Samuel Luke on behalf of Parliament. Northamptonshire was not part of the Eastern Association but was expected to contribute to the maintenance of the Newport garrison and it is Luke's correspondence which makes it clear what a very hard time the people of Daventry had during the Civil War.

(1) Bedfordshire Historical Record Society Vol. XXVII.
(2) Bedfordshire Historical Record Society Vol. XLII.

DAVENTRY (contd)

A SKIRMISH AT DAVENTRY

The first actual fighting which took place in the town was on 23 February 1645 when a detachment of Royalist soldiers, out plundering from Oxford, clashed with some Parliamentary horsemen already settled in the town. This worried the local population so much that five days later the Earl of Essex reported to Luke that the Northampton Committee had asked for protection and that he had sent Captain Andrews with his own troop of soldiers and two companies of dragoons to camp in a strategic position between Daventry and the Royalist stronghold at Oxford. Despite these precautions Luke's uncle sent a report to him on 25 March that the Royalist officer, Sir Marmaduke Langdale, had a brigade of soldiers quartering at Daventry; an expression which really meant living on what they could take from the countryside round about. There was no fighting in the town but the soldiers came and went joining in the minor struggles and sieges elsewhere.

DAVENTRY IN DANGER

It was in May that the people of Daventry suddenly found themselves in the desperately dangerous position of being an unprotected barrier between two nervously circling armies. On 8 May, King Charles and his army eventually left their winter headquarters at Oxford heading north apparently towards Chester. He was pursued by Lieutenant – General Oliver Cromwell but Parliament were not sure of the King's intentions and Cromwell was ordered to return south. Cromwell stayed at Daventry on 20 May. He was extremely short of money and could not buy all the food and supplies he needed for his men. He was very much against allowing any theft or damage being done by his soldiers and wrote a desperate letter to Luke saying that he was about to move on to Brackley – would Luke try and raise some money and send it on to him, so that he could pay his men and buy their essential supplies? Luke also received another letter, this time from one of his cousins written the day after Cromwell's. He suggested that Cromwell and his men would be staying at Daventry for a few more days while Parliament waited to see which way the King would move, but in fact Cromwell was in Oxford by 22 May. Soon afterwards he was sent to Cambridge to recruit more men. Daventry was left undefended and extremely vulnerable.

During the first ten days of June, following the King's brutal attack on Leicester on 1 June, Charles and his army marched around the central Midlands sometimes narrowly avoiding a large detachment of the Parliamentary Army under Major General Fairfax. Luke's correspondence shows just how close these two armies were to each other and how much the people of Daventry and district suffered during those days leading up to the Battle of Naseby.

KING CHARLES VISITS THE TOWN

Within the first few days of the month, Charles and his army arrived in the town, quite unaware that General Fairfax was only a mile away. On the seventh Charles visited Market Harborough but sent soldiers back to Daventry demanding more supplies. He returned the following day and on the ninth, the Parliamentary officer, Sir William Boteler, wrote to Luke reporting that the King was still staying in the town and that his men were out 'pillaging and plundering' the country round about. They had even gone to within half a mile of Northampton, rustling cattle and driving them back towards Daventry. A detachment of the Parliamentary army waited orders at Stony Stratford and on 11 June, Major Leonard Watson wrote that he and his soldiers had left that town and were marching towards Daventry because they had heard that the King was about to move. On the twelfth, scouts brought in messages that the King really was about to move and numerous letters were sent to Luke to keep him informed. He learned that Fairfax had sent a hundred soldiers to camp between Daventry and Banbury, with orders to keep watch over the roads leading out of the town. Sir Oliver Luke wrote that already these soldiers had captured some Royalist soldiers and were amazed to find how much stolen money and plunder they were carrying. One sergeant had been carrying £20. Parliamentary soldiers were being moved forward to within eight miles of Daventry and the King, realising that he would soon be forced to fight, had sent out into other counties to gather supplies and bring them to Daventry. Cromwell, who had arrived with his New Model Army at Bedford on 11 June, now moved on to join up with Fairfax at Kislingbury.

Charles eventually left his headquarters at the Wheatsheaf Inn on 13 June; he slept at Lubenham while his men camped at Market Harborough. The Parliamentary horsemen moved on and camped at Guilsborough and Naseby. One correspondent wrote to report that at times the opposing soldiers were 'lying within pistol shot of each other'. Sir John Norwich wrote from Rockingham to report that Charles had sent his soldiers out to bring in all available cattle and sheep and to bring in bacon, butter and salt and to leave these goods packed on waggons at Daventry ready to move on when needed. Three more reports came in; the following day Colonel Thomas Long reported that the King was back in Daventry and had led his troops up onto the high ground of Borough Hill. John Rushworth wrote that he and his soldiers were now within four miles of Daventry and that his scouts reported that the King's army had been 'standing-to' all-night. An unsigned letter reported that such Royalist soldiers as were getting in to Daventry were

DAVENTRY (contd)

transporting the King's 'plunder' off to Oxford.

Although King Charles knew that he was greatly outnumbered, he realised that he had now no choice but to fight. On 13 June, he left Daventry for the last time and moved to Market Harborough. The opposing army was camped just north of Naseby and so on 14 June the battle took place and King Charles was defeated.

KING CHARLES RECEIVED A WARNING

One reason given for the King's defeat was the the inefficiency of his scouts who failed to report that the Parliamentary soldiers were approaching nearer day by day.

There is a legend that on two successive nights a ghost appeared at the Wheatsheaf Inn and warned him to leave the district. The ghost is said to have been Thomas Wentworth, Earl of Strafford, friend and aide of the King but whom Charles had been obliged to execute, in 1647, because there was evidence of treason. Charles ignored the warning and according to tradition spent these important days out hunting in Fawsley Park.

Denton J13

VILLAGE PAINTINGS

St. Margaret's Church, which was rebuilt during 1827–28 is one of Northamptonshire's newer village churches, but nevertheless it boasts exceptionally fine wall paintings.

They were not started until 1970, when a local man, who was head scenic painter for the Old Vic and Sadler's Wells Theatres, began a series of elaborate murals. There are groups of figures representing secular events such as the women of the village resisting all attempts to remove the well on the village green. Scenes depict events in the history of St. Margaret's Church and biblical stories, where local people acted as models for the different characters.

A particularly attractive feature of the paintings is the inclusion, picture by picture, of different indigenous trees.

Dingley

THE STORY OF THE NUN'S BRASS

On the chancel wall of the now disused All Saints' Church is a brass depicting a kneeling woman at prayer. It is thought to be the latest brass of a nun to be found in Great Britain.

The words, inscribed below the figure, inform us that the lady is Anne Boroeghe, second daughter of Nycolas Boroeghe of Stanmer in the 'countye of Mydlesexe' and that she was 'sometyme professed in Clerkenwell nere London'. Anne Boroeghe died in April 1577, aged 75 years.

Her father, who died in 1527, some years before the Dissolution of the Monasteries, was buried in the Priory Church of St. Bartholomew's, Smithfield. At that time Anne was a nun, living in Clerkenwell, and her sister, Alys, was soon to marry a local man, Geffrey Chambers. It appears that when the Augustinian House at Clerkenwell was closed down in 1539 Anne was one of those professed nuns who was not only distressed by the loss of her secure religious household but also by the legal insistence that she should accept the break with Rome. Her niece Elizabeth, daughter of Alys, had married Sir Walter Stonor. In later years, the Stonors were registered as Roman Catholics. Her nephew, Alys' son, was a priest, who also found it difficult to abandon the faith of his ancestors.

Sir Walter died in 1550, and Elizabeth then married Edward Griffin, who was Attorney General to both Edward VI and his Roman Catholic sister, Queen Mary. Alys went to live at the Griffin's family house, Dingley Hall and it seems likely that Anne accompanied her, taking the £4 a year pension which she had been awarded on leaving Clerkenwell.

When Anne died, her family recorded on her brass '. . . the great losse' that poor people would feel '. . . who in dyverse wayes were by her relieved'.

Dodford

D13

'MAY ANGELS GUARD US . . .'

The Church of St. Mary is rich in medieval monuments, including a stone carving of a lady laying on a tomb chest with delicately carved angels surrounding her pillow. She is said to be Wentiliana of Keynes, daughter of Sir Robert of Keynes whose monument is carved in Purbeck marble. He is dressed as a knight and wears chain mail armour. Wentiliana died in 1376.

DODFORD (contd)

Nearby is an albaster monument to Sir John Cressy who died in 1444 having been knighted by Henry V. Two angels hold his shield and a group of angels and human mourners surround his tomb.

Dunstable E17

A TOWN AND ITS SCHOOLS

This town, which grew up on the crossing of two main roads more or less equally distant from London, Oxford and Cambridge, has always been lucky in its schools.

Originally, Dunstable was dominated by the Priory of Augustinian Canons. At this time early in the 12th century, a famous French scholar, Geoffrey de Gorham, had travelled to England to take up the position of schoolmaster at the prestigious Abbey School of St. Albans. Delayed by storms in the channel, he arrived too late and some time later he was advised by the Abbot that there was an opening for someone to start a school at King Henry I's new town of Dunstable. De Gorham moved into the town and appears to have been very successful.

At home in France he had seen religious plays performed at various times of the year. He decided that his schoolboys should put on what may be the first such play to be performed in England. It was based on the story of St. Catherine of Alexandria, who gave her name to the 'Catherine Wheel' – (firework). To give dignity to this performance, de Gorham borrowed the beautifully embroidered choir robes from his friends at St. Albans. We will never know whether the fire which took place at his home and completely destroyed these precious gowns was accidental or whether it was a deliberate attempt to prevent what some townspeople regarded as an act of sacrilege. It is recorded that the shocked and desperately distressed de Gorham gave up his profession as a schoolmaster and entered the abbey as a penitential monk. As the years went by he rose through the abbey hierarchy and in 1119 was elected Abbot. It seems likely that the Priory then took over the school; a 'school house' was recorded in South Street at the time of the Dissolution. When William Newton, who was chaplain at the Dunstable Fraternity, made his will in 1500, he left 1d. for each poor scholar.

A century after the closing of the Priory, Dunstable, which was owned by the Crown and administered by the Earl of Ailesbury at Ampthill, gradually came under the influence of the Marsh family, resident at Kingsbury. The daughter and granddaughters of William Marsh married wealthy city businessmen; although they lived in London, they adopted Dunstable, and their families are commemorated in Dunstable Priory Church.

In the 18th century there was a growing feeling that children should be given a solid grounding in religious education and should be taught the basic principles of reading and writing so that they could read the Bible, be capable of learning a trade or be able to handle money in a shop. When William Marsh's grandson, William Chew, died in 1712, his executors felt that money should be set aside to start a charity school in Dunstable. This came to fruition in 1715, when forty poor boys, who all had to be over seven years of age, able to read from the New Testament and attend Church on Sundays, were enrolled in the new school. They were given uniforms to wear while they attended the school, received a very good all-round education and when they left, at the age of 14, there was also some money set aside to help with their apprenticeships.

WORTHINGTON GEORGE SMITH

Although when Worthington Smith arrived in Dunstable in 1885 he came from London and was thought by some to be a newcomer to the area, his father's family had farmed land in the villages around Dunstable for several generations. His father had been born at Gaddesden Row but having entered the Civil Service had moved to London, so that Worthington George Smith was born on 23 March 1835 in Shoreditch. This was where he grew up and went to school but he spent many holidays at Gaddesden Row and got to know Dunstable and the surrounding villages with that intimate detail that only comes from childhood exploration.

Even as a boy his hobby was drawing old buildings and artifacts. By amazing good fortune he was apprenticed to the architect, A. E.

DUNSTABLE (contd)

Johnson, whose offices were in The Strand, and who sent him to the British Museum to study Greek and Roman sculpture, as part of his training. His highly specialised interests were encouraged by Sir Horace Jones with whom he finished his training.

Becomes An Architect

From this excellent start he was able to get an opening in the even more specialised profession of designing ecclesiastical furniture for the Roman Catholic Church, which led him to his interest in first drawing and later engraving the most intricate details of both plants and classical artifacts. His designs were in great demand, his financial position became easier and he was able to travel and build up an impressive portfolio of drawings.

In 1856 he married a Dunstable girl, Henrietta White, and soon they had a young family. Increasingly he was involved in the more everyday forms of architecture which he found very frustrating and he was only 26 when he resigned his position and began to build up a freelance business as an illustrator, using both his arts of drawing and engraving.

And Then A Botanist

His love of detail lifted his work far above the level of the average illustrator so that when he began to study fungi he found several commercial opportunities. Life with this absorbed scholar must at times have been very trying; on one occasion he brought home an unfamiliar species of toadstool and having studied and drawn them pronounced that they were safe to eat. His wife and two year old daughter only ate a little but even that was enough to cause such violent sickness that their doctor was seriously concerned. Worthington, who had eaten most of them himself, was seriously ill and was lucky to recover. This experience encouraged rather than frightened him and on several later occasions he tested for himself and on himself earlier reports that a plant was thought to be poisonous.

His articles and drawings were published in magazines and books; he published books of his own drawings and travelled around the country as a very popular lecturer. He would never be a rich man but the chance which had led him into a branch of architecture which in turn led to a study of plants, meant that he was able to enter the specialist market of writing and illustrating for the comparitively new subject of mycology. From this it was a short step into the study of plant diseases and recognition and commissions from the agricultural industry.

His Growing Interest In Archaeology

During the 1870's his interests turned towards archaeology and in particular to the worked flints that he found amongst the excavations which were taking place at Stoke Newington Common, near his Shoreditch home. It was there that he found his first 'Palaeolithic Man', in the layer, well below the present surface, where millions of years ago, in between the ice ages, the people known as 'Palaeolithic' or 'Old Stone Age', once lived. He described his discoveries in the Journal of the Anthropological Institute, in 1879.

A few years later chance again played a part.

He Moves To Dunstable

In 1884 his doctor diagnosed that his intermittent ill health was caused by a heart complaint and advised him to move out to the country. He visited his wife's home town of Dunstable and in a pile of gravel, alongside the road, he picked up a flake of flint which he recognised as being similar to those that he had found at Stoke Newington. In 1885 the Smith family moved to 'The Hawthorns', 121 High Street South, Dunstable – (pulled down in 1959).

This became not only the family home but the private museum for his more important finds (many of which are now in the British, Luton or other museums), a library for his books, a garden and conservatory for his rare plants and a place where he could entertain friends and colleagues from the world of Botany and Archaeology. He lived in High Street South for 32 years, until his death on 27 October 1917. During those years he continued his work as a writer, artist and engraver, now adding archaeology to his other subjects. He excavated two of the prehistoric burial mounds on Dunstable Downs (the skeletons uncovered are in the Luton Museum) and others elsewhere, he explored and recorded archaeological sites all around the area and all his notes and publications were accompanied by his accurate and detailed drawings. From time to time he identified and explored numerous of the Palaeolithic sites which had been his prime archaeological interest before he came to Dunstable.

Internationally he is probably best known for his exciting discovery at Caddington, in March 1890. For months he had been watching the excavators at work in the brick-clay pits and from time to time had been rewarded with evidence that the stone-age men, who had been forced to return to the warmer parts of the continent, when part of England was once again covered in ice, had indeed lived in this area. At the end of a long day in the fields he turned back to make one more check on a likely site and in the dusk he could just see worked flints sticking out of the clay. With such rising excitement that he cut his fingers, he loosened the razor sharp flints and carefully carried them home.

DUNSTABLE (contd)

His patience had been rewarded by the identification of a very rare manufacturing site, where the actual flint tools were made. In Dunstable he is better known for his book 'Dunstable, Its History and Surroundings', published in 1904* and for his discovery of the Charter which King Henry I gave to the town in 1131.

His Work Was At Last Rewarded

His work was recognised nationally in 1902, when he was awarded a Civil List pension of £50 per year. The following year the people of Dunstable rewarded him by making him the first Freeman of the Borough.

A readable and detailed account of his excavations, publications and his archaeological finds can be found in Bedfordshire Historical Record Society Volume LVII, written by local archaeologist James Dyer.

*Republished by Bedfordshire County Council in 1980.

Eaton Bray   C18

A FAMOUS KNIGHT

The name 'Eaton' comes from the descriptive Saxon name – a village partly surrounded by streams, but the 'Bray' suffix comes from a family who only lived in the village for less than a century.

At the time the barons were trying to persuade King John to sign the Magna Carta, the owner of this village was William de Cantilupe. Due to the unsettled conditions at the time he built a large defended Manor House (near the present Park Farm). This had a moat, gatehouse, its own chapel dedicated to St. Nicholas and stables for 60 horses.

Before the Civil War started, he began to plan a new church for the village, but it was completed by a later owner, Reginald Bray, who, it is said, was the knight who picked up the fallen crown from the dead King Richard III and put it onto the head of the future Henry VII. Certainly Henry knighted him, and in 1490, granted him the Manor of 'Eaton'.

A carved stone head high up on the exterior of St. George's Chapel, Windsor, is said to represent this famous knight. In his day he was a famous architect and St. George's Chapel was his most well-known design. He was responsible for the final design of the beautiful church of St. Mary's. On one of the stones in the south wall of the Lady Chapel, (a part of his original design remaining today) can be seen a mark in the shape of a hemp bray – a pun on his name.

Because Sir Reginald was childless when he died he was succeeded by his nephew Edmund who became Sir Edmund Bray of Eaton. There is a brass in the church commemorating Edmund's wife Jane, who died on 5 March 1539. She is depicted surrounded by her only son and ten daughters and wearing the elaborate clothes suitable for a lady in her position. The brass was originally on the chancel floor.

AN UNUSUAL CLERGYMAN

The Rev. John Hall Doe came to the village as vicar in 1871 and remained for 20 years, during which time the church became derelict and dangerous. He bred pedigree Berkshire pigs and, like many other local people, kept ducks. He was even prepared to act as village dentist when required. When 'Father' Doe (as he asked people to call him) came to the village he was extremely enthusiastic, held matins and evensong daily and four services each Sunday, but his form of service was far too High Church for his congregation who gradually left the church, which was already in a bad state of repair.

His apparently sudden decision to leave the village was announced by him halfway through the morning service when, in the middle of the sermon, he took off his surplice, flung it at the congregation, announced he was to become a Roman Catholic, walked out of the church and out of the village.

Ecton J12

THE BLACKSMITHS OF ECTON

The Franklin family was already settled in this village when the Ecton parish registers first started. Benjamin Franklin, the famous American inventor, whose father Josiah left Ecton in 1683, could trace his ancestors back for several generations among these pages. Several members of Franklin's family were blacksmiths. 'Franklin' gravestones can still be identified in the churchyard, where, beside the path, two flowering cherry trees were planted in the late 1960's by a descendant, Robert Franklin.

Elstow F9

EVERY PICTURE TELLS A STORY

The beautiful Abbey Church of St. Mary and St. Helena takes its double name from the dedication of the Benedictine Nunnery, 'The Abbey of St. Mary and St. Helena' which was founded by Judith, niece

ELSTOW (contd)

of King William I soon after 1076. Her husband, Waltheof, Earl of Huntingdon, had been one of the very few Saxon landlords who held land under the first Norman King. During 1076 he was executed for taking part in a rebellion against the king. It has been suggested that she founded the nunnery because of her remorse for having informed her uncle of his disloyalty.

There is a brass on the floor of the church which clearly shows the costume of Elizabeth Harvey, an early 16th century abbess. Abbess Elizabeth Boyvill surrendered her house on 16 August 1539 as part of the general movement to close all such religious houses and went to live with some of her nuns in Bedford. Eventually the empty house and the estate was purchased by Sir Thomas Hillersdon.

Elstow nuns had been the daughters and widows of wealthy families. Their lives had not been as physically hard or as strictly controlled as nuns in other religious houses. Instead of sleeping in cold, draughty cubicles, they had shared comfortable dormitories and had eaten in a warm, well-furnished dining room. Because of this Hillersdon did not pull down all of the building; some of the rooms were adapted and formed one wing of the new private house. The impressive front entrance stands to this day.

Several of the Hillersdon family were buried at Elstow and high on the church walls are the family hatchments. These painted boards, which show the family coats of arms, were placed on the coffin during the funeral procession and service, displayed at the house during the following year and then hung in the church.

On display in the nave is a picture of the old mansion house and a copy of an entry from the Parish Register recording the baptism of John Bunyan. Internationally, Elstow is known as the parish in which John Bunyan was born, baptised and grew up. Until he went to take part in the Civil War, c.1644, he lived with his family across the fields at Harrowden but when he returned, aged about 19 or 20, he married an equally young girl and eventually they settled down in a house near the present St. Helena Restaurant. (For the complete story of John Bunyan, Bedfordshire's most famous son, read 'John Bunyan, His Life And Times' by Vivienne Evans).

A RIOT AT ELSTOW

During the Summer of 1834 the new Vicar of the Abbey Church of St. Mary and St. Helena, the Rev. John Wing, arranged for his previous clerk from the parish of Stevington to officiate at Elstow. On Sunday, 27 July, this new clerk arrived early and was already in the official seat before the old clerk arrived. According to the Cambridge Chronicle, halfway through the service the dissatisfaction of the congregation '. . .

broke out into a complete uproar' followed by 'a scene of the most disgraceful description . . . which completely unmanned the Revd. gentleman and he was unable to proceed with the service'. The Elstow clerk complained to the Bishop but despite his support both clerks continued to attend the church '. . . both making the responses etc., as nearly together as possible'.

On Saturday, 16 August, a meeting was held at the Town Hall, Bedford, attended by S. Whitbread Esq., the Vicar, the Church Wardens and many of the congregation. Both sides put their case but no conclusion was arrived at and matters went from bad to worse ending in a court case, when, it was claimed. '. . . on 13th day of October at parish of Elstow (the congregation) unlawfully riotiously did assemble together to disturb the peace'. Apparently the service was brought to a violent end and for over an hour they shouted, fought and threw 'diverse stones and other hard substances at and against the said church and through certain windows . . . and upon one John Wing . . . clergyman . . . in the performance of the sacred duty of his function as a clergyman . . .'.

According to the evidence they had succeeded in terrifying poor John Wing and damaged ten panes of glass to the value of £9. Despite this they were found not guilty.

Eydon

SOME TALES TOLD BY A COUNTRYMAN

Mr. Sydney Tyrrell, 'Old Syd' to his friends, decided to set down a record of his family's history in the hope that it would inspire his grandchildren to take an interest in their ancestors. He admitted that he had left it too late to write a detailed village history but luckily he realised how important it is to gather up village stories and record them before they are lost.

Included in 'A Countryman's Tale', are interesting snippets from the Parish Registers, where he discovered that on 30 January 1623, the vicar had baptised 'John Hinton the sonne of Henry Hinton of the Graynge and Jane Warde whome he gott with chylde being his mayde'. Also that on 29 October 1642 'One Birminham soulder of ye King's army and wounded at ye battel of Edgehill was buryed with us'. Presumably some mortally wounded soldier who had managed to whisper the name of his home town before being laid to rest in this peaceful churchyard.

THE SUFFERINGS OF THE QUAKERS

In the British Library is the original of a very old book 'The Sufferings of the Quakers'. In the 17th century these innocent people were shamefully treated by the authorities, and local 'correspondents' kept records of the worst offences against them. In his research Tyrrell uncovered the story of a local Quaker who lived in Eydon in the mid 17th century.

In 1654 a man called Thomas Smallbone walked the 10 miles into Banbury, to learn for himself more about this new movement of people who he had heard were meeting in that town. He was converted to their ideas and as this was during the time of Parliamentary control, when such movements were quite legal, he was quite within the law. However, he refused to pay his share of the rates required for the upkeep of St. Nicholas Church. Four years later his debt had risen to £3. 5 shillings (£3.25p), and within less than two years Charles II would be invited to become King and the rules of the Church of England would again be enforced by law. Knowing the sympathy of the local magistrates, the rector, John Parkes B.D., felt secure enough to take Smallbone to court. For refusing to pay the £3. 5 shillings, the magistrates sent him to prison for five weeks and impounded goods to the value of 9 shillings.

Smallbone was not the only Quaker in the parish, as soon after the Coronation of Charles II, the Rev. Parkes wrote to Parliament to report that the number at Eydon and his other parish of Culworth were causing him great concern.

THE CELEBRATORY MILESTONE

The safe arrival of a baby daughter is invariably a very great blessing, especially in the 18th century when infant mortality was still so high, but few families have been able to celebrate the event by building an obelisk in the middle of the road! In 1789, Sir English Dolben, of Finedon Hall, had this milestone built to celebrate 'the many blessings of 1789'.

The whole country had been extremely anxious as King George III had suffered one of his distressing bouts of mental illness from October 1788 until it lifted in February 1789. The statement announcing his complete recovery was made during the first week in March. On 23 April, there was a three hour service in St. Paul's Cathedral to celebrate his recovery. Other celebrations took place around the country and a special medal was struck to mark his restoration to health. Today his symptoms of madness are considered to be one of the symptoms of the illness Porphyria.

King George's youngest sister, Louisa, died during 1789, and this daughter, their fifth, who was born to John English Dolben and his wife Hannah, was baptised 'Louisa' in the same year.

'I Do Not Like Thee Dr. Fell'

One of the more colourful of the Dolben family was John, founder of the Finedon branch of the family. He was a loyal Royalist during the Civil War and then returned to teach at Christ Church College, Oxford, was ordained and rose to become Bishop of York.

On the north wall of St. Mary's Church is a triple picture, painted by Lely in 1803. One of the gentlemen is John Dolben himself, one Richard Allestry and the third is John's friend, the infamous Dr. Fell.

FLITWICK WATER

On 24 April 1948 a meeting of the Bedfordshire Natural History Society was held on Flitwick Moor. They had invited Dr. (later Sir) Henry Godwin, from the Botany Department of Cambridge University, to discuss with them the possibility of an ecological survey being made to find out more about this important site. From then on Flitwick Moor was recognised as a rare site for the study of peat soil, plants with a tolerance of different depths of water and the forms of water life tolerant of the peat-water. The Beds. and Hunts. Wildlife Trust took an interest in the site and since 1969 they have leased and directly managed an increasing area of the moor. Each year they hold open days when their work can be seen and demonstrated to the public.

By the standards of other peat moors, Flitwick is comparitively modern. Dr. Godwin suggested that the water had gradually drained from the marsh into channels or streams, leaving the peat behind to dry out, over the last 2,000 years. Over the centuries farmers have deliberately dug channels and drained the land, and the so-called moor, which has always been privately owned and not open common land, has been cultivated and mainly used for farming. The areas which were solid peat were also of value because each year thousands of turves were dug for fuel. Although the local people may have recognised that the water which divided the different areas of peat had medicinal properties, there is no documentary evidence of this until c.1790.

Dr. Rodomonte Dominicetti

A Dr. Bartholomew Dominicetti caused something of a stir in London by opening a 'hot bath' house alongside his fashionable house in Cheyne Walk, Chelsea. It quickly became popular and for a time was one of the ingredients of fashionable London life. His son, (Dr.) Rodomonte, who claimed to have trained at the University of Padua, opened a more sophisticated establishment at Panton Square in the Haymarket. His main bath had a spring running in and out of it but he had also arranged warm and hot baths on the Roman principle. Although it was well planned and advertised and by the standards of the day quite hygienic, it was expensive to run. It appears that high prices together with the usual fickleness of fashion, caused him to go bankrupt.

He had married a girl from Ampthill and so when they were obliged to leave London they stayed in the town while they looked around for new premises. Shortly afterwards they bought a house there and Dr. Dominicetti set up a practice. Little is known about his stay in Ampthill but he must have had baths of some sort or another. His medical success was so great that he decided to find larger premises where he could provide more varied treatments. Some time before 1790 he heard about the unusual Flitwick Moor and someone must have told him that the water which drained into the channels had medicinal properties. He took a long lease on East End House (long since disappeared) and opened it as a nursing home. He produced a pamphlet explaining that his practice had outgrown his Ampthill premises and that at Flitwick he had been able to '. . . erect a neat and convenient apparatus for the Preparation and Application of his various artificial Medicated Water, Vaporous and Dry Baths'. Not only was he trying to attract local custom but he was also trying to attract paying guests. He described the grounds, the nearby mill stream, the kitchen gardens, the good roads and the stage coach which left the Cross Keys, St. John Street, London, three times a week. He offered to accommodate ladies and gentlemen by the quarter or by the year. They could even cook for themselves if they preferred. Although he made use of '. . . artificial Medicated Water' he does not seem to have exploited the chalybeate water for which Flitwick would later become famous. By the time of his death on 9 December 1817 he had left Flitwick and had been living in London for several years.

Henry King Stevens

The years went by and nothing more was written that would connect Flitwick and its water with the medical profession. Then just before 1860 Mr. Stevens, who was tenant of a small estate known as 'The Folly', became aware of the fact that one or more of the springs on his land rose straight out of the peat and as he knew that there was a market for spring water with medicinal properties, he presumably tried samples of his spring water on his family and friends. The fame of his 'bottled water' spread and there was soon a local market for Flitwick water. People were quite prepared to pay 2d. (roughly 1p) a bottle to use as a tonic or medicine for indigestion but soon the water got a reputation for being helpful in healing open sores. Stevens was very anxious to receive medical approval for his spring water so that he could expand his market. Repeatedly he sent samples to various doctors and influential people and eventually in 1885 he succeeded; Flitwick Water won the major prize at the National Health Society's Exhibition. Tests were made and analysis of the water showed that not only was there a high level of ferric oxide in the water but that it was in a form that was easily absorbed by the body and did not cause constipation. An article in the Lancet commended the water and suggested that it should be taken with lemonade. At last Stevens had the recommendations that he needed and he opened an office and warehouse in London and took on extra staff at Flitwick to collect and bottle the water. Just as he was in sight of success

FLITWICK (contd)

he died, aged 62. His daughters approached the man who held a mortgage on the property and together they put the estate and mineral water business up for auction.

R. W. White and Co.

This company, whose lemonade and other soft drinks are still well known today, were the highest bidders. They formed The Flitwick Chalybeate Company and expanded the business; having got recommendations from various doctors and hospitals they persuaded chemists to stock it as well as shops and railway buffets. The collection of the water became more hygienic, the degree of iron salts was more or less controlled. Tanks, pumps and siphons were installed at Flitwick and the water was transported to London by train, in 10 gallon containers. During the 1920's, White's and other such companies found that artificially produced fruit drinks were gaining in popularity and were cheaper to produce than bottled water which had to be transported from one place to another. The business decreased but it was as late as 1938 that it was finally sold, the buildings dismantled and The Folly, which had become the manager's house, was taken down.

Fotheringhay   N4

AN HISTORIC CASTLE

The remains of an historic castle still stand here. It is thought to have been built by Simon de Sentes, first Earl of Northampton and Huntingdon, although Edmund Langley (son of Edward III) rebuilt most of the main structures.

Richard III, great grandson of Prince Edmund, was born at the castle. However, it is better known as the place where Mary Queen of Scots was imprisoned and then executed in 1587. There is a plaque on the ruins which records the event. A clump of very large thistles, which are traditionally said to be descended from Scottish thistles planted at her request, are said to grow near the ruins.

POLITICAL THOUGHTS AT FOTHERINGHAY

In the early months of 1939 the well-known travel writer, H. V. Morton, set out to put together 'The Record of a Journey Before The War, and After The Outbreak of War'.

By the time that he arrived at Fotheringhay war was only weeks away, and for the first time he saw a notice giving instructions as to the

proceedings to be adopted following the outbreak of war. These started with the order that church bells would not be rung for services until the end of the war and ended with the order not to rush to the spot where a bomb had dropped, just to 'see what it looks like' and 'not to be surprised at anything that may happen'.

He stayed at The Falcon where he met a professor of history. Morton tried to strike up a conversation concerning the war news in the morning papers. 'I know nothing about it' replied the historian. 'I gave up reading the papers last September and feel better for it in every way'. So they began to talk about Mary Queen of Scots and the 'callous cruelty' of her murder. Morton's point of view was, that, in 1939, it was very difficult to come to terms with such barbaric behaviour in the distant past. The professor, however, felt that during the years following the 1914–18 war, there had been such a marked drop in moral values that he did not find it difficult to imagine. 'Danger' he said 'produces fear, and fear produces unscrupulousness. Money and fear of Catholic Spain were two great factors in Elizabethan politics. Money and the fear of Nazi Germany' he said were the great factors in the England of 1939. The people of 1939, he said, were shocked by the brutal acts of some continental politicians, even if their leaders were not, and he reminded Morton that leaders did not necessarily lead forward but could also lead backwards. The only hope for the world was for the people to band together and refuse to be led backwards to the brutality of the 16th century.

Geddington

THE ELEANOR CROSSES

Of the twelve crosses which Edward I ordered to be erected in memory of his queen, Eleanor of Castile, only three survive and two of these are in Northamptonshire.

The one which stands to the south of Northampton, near Delapre Park, has been much altered, but the other one, which stands in the centre of this village, although repaired, has not lost its original design. It is now in the care of English Heritage.

Queen Eleanor died on 28 November 1290, and on 4 December King Edward led a funeral procession back to London. Most of the overnight stops were at religious houses, and at Delapre they spent the night at the nunnery, but there was once a most comfortable royal hunting lodge standing next to the Geddington churchyard. This lodge was well known to King Edward; on several occasions he had used it to enjoy a few days hunting. The staff were used to entertaining large royal house parties, so it made a most suitable stop between Stamford and Northampton.

Guilsborough

THE CHURCHWARDEN'S ACCOUNTS

Sometime during the weeks following Easter, members of the Church of England meet together and elect representatives to hold the various positions necessary for the smooth running of the church during the year to come. The role of churchwarden is a responsible and varied one and its duties change from time to time in the same was as the church's role changes within the community.

Things that were taken for granted by the churchwardens of the 17th and 18th centuries would come as something of a shock in the late 20th century. If today's churchwarden, male or female, opened the front door and found a small boy standing there with a dozen dead sparrows or a man standing waiting, expecting a reward for handing over the tail of a dead fox, they would be somewhat startled if not downright shocked!

A surprising number of the account books kept by churchwardens throughout the centuries have survived. A selection taken from the Guilsborough books of the early 18th century include:-

Spares (Sparrows)	– reward	2d.
A Hedgehog	– reward	2d.
Paid for 2 young urchins (baby hedgehogs)		4d.
Paid for a fox		1s. 0d.
Beer for the men mending the lead on the church roof		2s. 6d.
A new set of bell ropes		11s. 6d.
To the bell ringers on November 5th		4s. 0d.
To the 'geys' (mummers) on November 5th		2d.
To prayer books and 'a book of orders for infected cattle'*		4s. 0d.
To the bell ringers for celebrating the declaration of peace after the war with France and Spain		3s. 6d.
For a copy of an Act of Parliament 'against Profain cursing and swearing'		8d.
New lock between church and steeple		2s. 6d.
Some fine Holland cloth to mend the collar of a surplice		4d.
For repairs and washing of surplice		3s. 0d.
Thread and buttons for surplice		6d.

*Dated 1745 this is an exceptionally early example of an Act to control the spread of disease in cattle.

Harrold — B5

AGRICULTURAL PRICE REVIEW – 1308

A large agricultural estate of 200 acres known as Swanton belonged to the Knight Templars. They had been founded during the first Crusade to protect the Holy Land, but their land was taken back by the Crown in April 1308. An inventory was drawn up which provides us with some very useful prices. These are very similar to those of Grove Priory (see Leighton Buzzard).
N.B. 2½p. = 6d. and 5p. = 1 shilling.

Household:

Eggs were valued by the score (20)	at 1¼d. per score
Hens, ducks and goslings	at 1½d. each
1 bushel of salt	at 6½d.

HARROLD (contd)

Field Work:

Blacksmith – shoeing 2 cart horses	1s. 1½d.
Blacksmith – making 3 iron plough shares	5¼d.
Carpenter repairing ploughs 7 working days	1s. 2d. (2d. per day)
Grazing 18 oxen (for the year)	3s. 0d.

In The Kitchen:

1 Bronze Pot	6s. 8d.
Trivet	2d.
Bowl	2d.
Grid Iron	3d.
3 Stools	6d.
Handmill for mustard	3d.
8 vats	1s. 6d.
1 tun	3d.
Pestle and mortar	3d.
Dough board	2d.
Sistern in furnace (for hot water?)	1s. 6d.

In The Pantry:

4 chests	2s. 0d.
2 barrels	1s. 0d.
3 troughs	1s. 3d.
3 casks	3s. 0d.
1 tub	3d.

THE VILLAGE SCHOOLMASTER

In both 1717 and 1720 the Bishop of Lincoln required his official 'visitors' to enquire about schools which were available to the poor people of each parish. On neither occasion did they find one in Harrold. The first time that one was recorded was in 1818 when the vicar, Henry Dixon, reported to a Select Committee of Parliament that, although there was no charity school available for the children of his 796 parishioners, there were two or three little private schools for middle class children. The majority of the children were employed in lace-making.

The Church of St. Andrews had started a Sunday School which provided simple lessons of reading and writing based on the prayer book, Bible and other such books, and there was such a great demand that nearly one hundred children attended and had to be divided into two sessions.

These Sunday Schools were for children whose parents were members of the Established Church, and many Nonconformists in both counties were very concerned about the education of their own children, so they soon provided a similar but Bible-based form of education, which was open to all. By 1833, the Harrold Independent Sunday School was teaching 138 children in addition to just over one hundred who were attending at St. Andrews.

The number of private schools supported by parents had also grown. Nearly 50 small children (24 boys and 25 girls) were attending the three infant schools, but the need for girls to work in the lace industry can still be seen. Once they had left the infant schools, only 11 girls continued into the private day schools compared with 41 boys.

In this village, as elsewhere, the vicar and Parochial Church Council grew concerned at the number of children who were receiving a form of education which did not include study of the Prayer Book and Catechism. Proper school buildings were put up and, in addition to the 35 boys and 69 girls who attended on Sundays, 78 boys were now enrolled as weekday scholars and there was a special class on Sunday evenings for 11 older boys.

This school was not built with comfort in mind. Until a new stove was installed in late October 1863, on cold winter days the children's hands were too cold to hold a pen! The new stove wasn't entirely successful because of the smoke which, on windy days, poured back into the school room. On very windy days they had to put the fire out altogether, abandon writing and fill in the time with more active lessons.

The poor teacher had a very difficult time at the school. The children came from terribly poor families who desperately missed their potential earnings and resented the weekly payment of school pence: 2d. for the first child and 1d. each for the others.

Few of the children could see any future benefits from schooling and many were awkward and difficult. The farmers and other employers who should have been supporting them openly encouraged the boys to stay away when the seasonal work came round. The health of the mothers was often poor and with the arrival of each new baby the older girls were obliged to stay at home and look after mother, baby and toddlers. The vicar, the Rev. Garde frequently came into the school to make sure that Prayer Book services were held and that the Catechism was taught while the Nonconformist parents threatened to remove their children if they were not excused from this denominational instruction. As with all such schools there was trouble with the drains and on 11 January 1864, the vicar came into school to complain that the boys were using the front of the school as a urinal.

Not only were the boys and girls kept at home to work, but at a time when life was so hard for children, they took every opportunity to attend where there was free entertainment. On 4 July 1863, many of the children went across to Pavenham to join in the Temperance Fete and on 19 May 1864 they went to Odell fair. When the entertainment was to

HARROLD (contd)

be held in the village, such as Harrold's own fair on 10 May, the master would close the school. He must have been very hurt when his authority was undermined by the farmers who employed the boys as beaters or when the vicar had some of the choristers in church on St. Andrews Day.

When we read in the School Log Book that on 1 April 1864 the teacher punished several (children) for talking and laughing, it being April Fool's Day, it seems rather harsh. However, looking back through the previous year's entries one can see that he was having a very hard time. There were constant references to vandalism and what we would regard as very petty thefts. One boy was punished severely and the whole school cautioned 'against so great a sin' because he had stolen ½d. from another scholar. Seen as a quarter of the other boy's 'school money', the 2d. a week which his parents had to pay towards his schooling, the offence was actually serious. In the October of 1864, the master was most annoyed when he found that one boy had slipped two farthing coins into the pile of school money, pretending that they were two halfpennies. This master struggled on until Christmas 1865.

As Henry Marchant, who took over in January, commented on the low attainment of the children and the poor discipline, it is possible that the previous teacher may have been a poor disciplinarian; he undoubtedly had troubles with his assistant staff. However, there is no doubt that he was himself an excellent scholar and had he come to Harrold 20 years later, when education was well established, he would have had a much easier time. Although most of his pupils were desperate to get away from school and out to work in jobs from which there would be little chance of advancement, the master was anxious to help the older boys learn skills which would take them into the more skilled professions. Individual boys were offered Latin, book-keeping and shorthand, while in addition to reading, writing and Bible Stories, a lot of the children were taught grammar, spelling and arithmetic, and the older ones studied history and geography.

Harrowden K10

THE LOST EARL

This complicated family saga starts with a Norman adventurer, William Algernon, who arrived in faraway Yorkshire during 1067. He married the daughter of a dispossessed Saxon landowner and together they founded the renowned northern family of Percy.

Famous for their defence against warring Scottish raiders at home,

and against the French at Crècy and Poitiers in 1377, the 4th Lord Percy was rewarded by being created Earl of Northumberland.

During the reign of Queen Elizabeth I, the family fell from royal favour, because they refused to abandon their belief in the Pope and the Roman Catholic form of worship.

Living so far north, the family managed to survive the upheavals of the 17th century Civil War, but finally the male line came to an end in May 1670. The vast estates were inherited by Lady Elizabeth Percy, daughter of the last Earl, and Charles II conferred the Earldom on to her stepbrother, George Fitzroy, illegitimate son of the last Earl.

Less than five months later, a 57 year old Irish merchant, called James Percy, arrived to claim both the title and the estates. Unfortunately, although he was quite convinced that he was the rightful heir, he had little actual proof and wasn't even certain which of the many male Percys was his great grandfather. Although the Percys were a famous northern family, the story that he told involves both Harrowden (near Wellingborough) and Pavenham in North Bedfordshire.

James Percy's story was that when the family were in trouble during the reign of Queen Elizabeth I and feared reprisals after the rebellion headed by the Earls of Northumberland and Westmorland in 1569, his great grandfather had decided to smuggle his children south to safety.

HARROWDEN (contd)

James' grandfather, Henry, his great uncle, Robert, and his two great aunts, all very young children at the time of the story, were packed into panniers and sent to a distant member of the family, Dame Vaux of Harrowden, slung on the back of a packhorse.

Unfortunately, James Percy was so vague about the details of his story, and so naive when it came to approaching possible witnesses, that his case dragged on for many years, ending with a planned hearing at the House of Lords. At each stage in his investigation he had given Lady Elizabeth Percy plenty of warning about his plans and so, on each occasion, written evidence would disappear or witnesses would change their evidence. So confused was James Percy that he decided that the details of his original story were wrong and changed his story half way through the enquiry. As a result the House of Lords cancelled the hearing and declared him an imposter. So, after nearly 13 years, Percy was obliged to give up his claim and return to obscurity.

Quite apart from the tale of a lost inheritance within one of England's most well-known historic families, the thought of a family of small children, (including the heir to a famous Earldom), being smuggled into a Northamptonshire household, and growing up incognito, is well worth investigating. If the story is true, and it may well be so, because there are contemporary 'Percy' entries in the parish registers of Pavenham and Cogenhoe (near Harrowden) then what happened to the children? Did one of them, or one of their descendants, travel to Ireland?

In time to include the results of his research in the first volume of the Bedfordshire Magazine, C. D. Linnell searched through the local registers and dipped into the Percy family archives. The first question that he put to himself was:- If the children were delivered to Harrowden why did the name 'Henry Percy' turn up in the Pavenham parish register, over the county border?

Dame Vaux and her family were also Roman Catholics and before her marriage she had lived at Pavenham where she still owned land. It certainly seems likely that, for their own safety, she may have boarded them with her quiet and unassuming Roman Catholic tenants, where they were less likely to be found. It may have been James Percy himself who searched through the Pavenham register and marked it with a red, pointed hand.

Then Linnell set out to find if there was an Irish connection. He found that the 'James, son of Henry' had been baptized at Pavenham in 1581 and that he did indeed go to Ireland, but that they had died without leaving any surviving children. The 'Henry, son of Henry' whom James claimed to be his own father, had stayed in England and married a Northants girl called Lydia Cope. He found the entry of the marriage in Horton Parish Register dated 1614. However, some years later, Henry had deserted Lydia and her children, and gone to live in London with one of his mother-in-law's maids!

Lydia had had several children baptized in All Saints' Church, Harrowden. Henry was eight years old when his father ran off to London and probably 10 or 11 when his step-brother, William, was born to his grandmother's maid. Friends of Lady Elizabeth Percy produced William to try to confuse the case. Linnel discovered that this Henry (2) had crossed to Ireland, where he had joined his uncle James and in 1654 had inherited his estate, so the claimant, James, was indeed the son of Henry (2) (who was born in Pavenham) son of Henry (1), but, was this first Henry the heir to the Percy Earldom, who, back in 1569, had arrived in Harrowden hidden in a pannier?

Higham Ferrers M10

When Viscount Torrington visited this town he stayed at the Green Dragon. He was pleased to find that they had recently added some new stables. He does not record the charges made for this stabling but his over-night hotel bill was:-

Breakfast	9d.
Dinner	1s. 6d.
Wine	2s. 6d.
Breakfast	3d.

5s. 0d. shillings (25p.)

Higham Gobion J13

THE LITERARY SCHOLAR

The famous scholar, Professor Edmund Castell DD, was rector here for the last 20 years of his long life. He was in his 80th year when he was buried at St. Mary's Church, on 5 January 1685. His memorial, which he designed himself, gives a clue to his extraordinary knowledge of languages.

It is said that he wrote the closing words in 1674, when he first came to live in the village. Translated from their original Arabic, they read:-

'Living here he chose to be buried
In hopes of a better place than this'.

Born in Cambridgeshire, he received his MA in 1628, the year that John Bunyan was born. Unlike Bunyan he was happy within the Church

HIGHAM GOBION (contd)

of England and in 1666 was chaplain to Charles II. At different times he held academic positions at two Cambridge colleges and was a prebendary of Canterbury Cathedral but the main interest of his academic life was his Lexicon Heptaglotton covering Hebrew, Chaldee, Syriac, Samaritan, Ethiopic, Arabic and Persian. He published his Lexicon as a series of volumes but he cannot have expected to make a great deal of money out of such a specialised subject, especially as he was obliged to employ several young assistants at his own expense. However he cannot have foreseen the problems he would encounter.

Storage of the printed and bound copies proved to be extremely difficult. At least three hundred were destroyed in the Great Fire of London and two hundred were too soiled to be of any use. He moved them from one storehouse to another. When one warehouse owner went bankrupt, Castell hired waggons and drivers and moved his precious volumes into an empty house in Wimbledon and various other emergency storehouses. When he eventually returned to fetch the volumes from Wimbledon, the majority had been damaged by rats!

Nevertheless, a considerable number did survive to be sold or given away, and Castell bequeathed a hundred to the Bishop of London.

Hockliffe D16

THE BELL INN, HOCKLIFFE – IN RECEIPT OF STOLEN GOODS

On 17 December 1868, William Perry (a delivery man working for Mr. G. Bates, the miller of Park Street, Luton) was charged with stealing a quantity of split beans from his master's storehouse and selling them to William North at the Bell Inn, Hockliffe.

Bates noticed that his supply of beans was diminishing too quickly and began to suspect Perry of theft. Before he could bring a charge against his employee, he had to have proof. One bag of beans looks much like another, and he realized that a clever thief could soon dispose of the sacks. He had to find a way of identifying his own beans.

One night, he thoroughly mixed some black and white oats and some chaff into the top sack of beans and skilfully put his initials inside the sack, where they wouldn't be noticed. The next morning he followed Perry as he travelled out on his round and noticed that he made an unauthorized stop at Hockliffe. Bates immediately fetched a constable and caught Perry still at the inn.

Having demanded to search the landlord's barn, the constable soon found the suspect sack. When both the landlord and Perry denied all knowledge of it, the sack was opened, revealing the chaff and oat mixture. Jane, the publican's daughter, was a quick-thinking girl, cleverly explaining that Perry had pulled into the yard for a quick drink and asking her to mix up a feed for his horses, she had simply put a mix of feed-stuffs that were easily available into the sack.

Turning to the constable, Bates told him where to look for his initials inside the sack, and there, of course, they were. Perry finally admitted the offence, said he had never done anything like it before and swore it would be the last. The landlord confirmed his story and added that no money had changed hands – only free beer and tobacco. Although Bates did not know of the extent of the involvement of the Bell, he did know that Perry had been stealing small amounts for some time and insisted on a prosecution. Perry not only lost his job and his character but was committed to the Assizes.

Holdenby F11

HOLDENBY HOUSE

Holdenby House was built for Sir Christopher Hatton, who was Lord Chancellor at the time of Queen Elizabeth I, at which time it was thought to be the largest house in England. Partly because of his love of music and dancing, he was a great favourite of the Queen, and she visited Holdenby in 1583.

He also owned Kirby Hall and as, after his death, his heir, the third Sir Christopher, could not afford two such expensive mansions, he sold Holdenby to James I. In 1651, when Parliament was in control of the country, the house was sold to Captain Adam Baynes but it turned out that his intention was to pull it down and sell the bricks to developers, who were building in Northampton. Only the two great gate arches and the kitchen wing were left standing. The latter was enclosed within the new, and very much smaller house which was built in 1873.

HOLDENBY (contd)

King Charles' Garden

The gardens also survived the demolition, but because of their neglect most of their Elizabethan beauty was lost. However, a new garden has been created using plants of the type which would have been there during the 17th century.

Houghton Regis   E17

SAELIG HOUGHTON

Houghton the Saxon settlement on, or at the foot of the hill, had the suffix 'Regis' by the time of the Domesday Survey, 1086. Although this may have been to identify it because of the Houghton (later Conquest) near Ampthill, there is a strong tradition that the Saxons gave it the prefix 'Saelig' which usually meant fortunate. It was fortunate, because as a household manor of the King it was extremely prosperous, and although the farmers had quite a lot of dry, chalky soil on one side of the village, they also had all the land which stretched around three sides of what is now Dunstable crossroads.

THE HAMLETS

Sewell

In All Saints Church is a stone effigy of a Knight, Sir John Sewell. Edith, wife of Edward the Confessor had separated that piece of land from the rest of the village and used it as a reward for her servant, Walraven. The de Sewell family lived there until the last Sewell heiress married Edmund Dyve of Bromham.

Thorn

The Norman kings owned the rest of Houghton up until Henry I founded a town, Dunstable, on the crossroads (c.1100) and had built a royal residence for himself on one corner and a Priory for Augustinian canons on another. He gave the canons a share of the land at Houghton. He then rented the rest of the land (except the church land) to a Norman baron, called Hugh de Gurnay. The manor house was on the north side of the church and these two new tenants were always quarrelling as to who was Lord of the Manor. On one occasion Hugh de Gurnay sent his men to completely destroy the manor house and built himself a new one, complete with moat, at Thorn.

Calcutt

The Prior was so incensed that he travelled to Westminster and followed the King, wherever he went, until he got permission to build a similar house and moat, at Calcutt, on the border of Chalgrave.

Bidwell – An Important Christian Site

Saelig did not only mean fortunate, it sometimes meant peaceful or holy. When the Domesday statistics were collected, Houghton Regis had one of only four churches in Bedfordshire which owned land for its own support. Approximately sixty acres were recorded and from later maps these can be identified as laying in a long strip, behind the present church, bounded on the west by today's Bidwell Hill and on the east by what was then the King's home farm. The northern boundary of the church land is not so easy to identify. During the last few years, several pieces of information have been published, which, put together, give cause for thought about the importance of this land in the history of the Christian church in this country.

We know that the prehistoric people who lived on Puddlehill were pagan, as were the Roman soldiers who marched over the hill and forced the local people to build the roads and the new town of Durocobrivae. We also know that England's first Christian Martyr died, c.209, at nearby Verulamium, the city from which this area was controlled and administered. This, of course, is now the diocesan city of St. Albans.

Thanks to the efforts of the Manshead Archaeological Society, foundations have been excavated, slightly to the north of the later church land, which seem likely to have been an early Christian church. Traditionally, the name of what appears to be the boundary, 'Bidwell,' has been associated with a holy well, dedicated to St. Brigid, an Irish Saint who died c.524. In 1986, Patricia Bell, recently retired as archivist of the County Record Office, recorded that in 1225/6 the name was 'Holewellehulle' – see her book 'Belief in Bedfordshire'. So we have the possibility of a Roman church, a Saxon holy well or spring, a most unusual gift of land by some unknown Saxon King and an independent church already standing before the Norman Conquest, all in the same small area of this large rambling village.

Tithe Farm

Henry I gave this church land to his illegitimate son, Robert Earl of Gloucester. He gave it to St. Albans Abbey who jealously guarded it from both of the other two landlords. It is recorded that John Moore, who was Abbot of St. Albans from 1396 to 1401, had a 'good grange' built near the church with a '. . . foundation of stone, of timber and earth, well tiled and enclosed . . . with a strong wall'. This may well have been the origins of the tithe barn which was demolished in 1964.

Ickwell

THE FATHER OF ENGLISH CLOCKMAKERS

The clock on Northill Church was made in the 17th century by Thomas Tompion, but whether this was the man who lived nearby, or his more famous son, who moved on to London, is not known.

Thomas Junior was born in the thatched cottage which still stands on Ickwell Green, in 1639, and grew up in the village. When he was 27 he started a seven year apprenticeship in London, followed by a further two years as a journeyman. During this latter period he met a certain Dr. Hooke, who had drawn up plans for an entirely new form of pocket watch, controlled by a delicate spring mechanism.

Once Tompion had become established as a Master Clockmaker, in his own right, on the corner of Fleet Street and Water Lane, Hooke persuaded him to make up a watch to this new, intricate design. It proved to be a great success.

Hooke introduced him to Charles II who was so impressed with the delicacy and accuracy of Tompion's work that in 1676, he ordered him to make the accurate clocks needed for the Royal Observatory.

By the time of Tompion's death, in 1713, he was regarded as the finest watchmaker in England, so his body was not returned to Northill Church but was buried in the nave of Westminster Abbey. However, The Worshipful Company of Clockmakers have had a plaque put up in Northill Church, dedicated to 'The Father of English Clockmakers'.

Islip
M8

HENRY MACKLIN'S BRASSES

This interesting church, dedicated to St. Nicholas, is perhaps best known for its crocketed (crocket being a small ornament, usually a bud or a curled leaf, applied to the sloping side of the spire) spire, but inside, on the chancel floor, are large brasses designed by the Rev. Herbert Macklin, author of two of the standard books on brasses. 'Brasses of England' and 'Monumental Brasses'.

EXPERIMENT WITH COCOA

The Headmaster of Church End School, Kempston, reported on 9 February 1896 that, at the suggestion of the chairman of the Kempston School Board (Mr. E. Ransom), he had been trying an experiment of offering to provide a cup of hot milk, flavoured with cocoa and sugar, to each child prepared to pay 1d. per week. On the first Monday forty children provided 3/4d. Cocoa for the week cost 1/6d., milk 7½d., sugar 10d., leaving a profit of 4½d. The kettle was provided by the school board, while the cocoa was made by the pupil-teachers. The profit was used to buy biscuits to reward the 'little co-operators'. 'I am a firm believer', said the Headmaster 'in the old fashioned maxim, "stomach first, head next". Unless I am much mistaken, England in the future will want strong men of muscle as well as of brain to protect the interests of our mighty empire. Every little helps'.

A FAMOUS FAMILY OF BELL-FOUNDERS

The Eayre family, many of whom were Quakers, had been settled in Kettering for some generations before the birth of Thomas (1) the first of the family to make a living as a bell-founder. He was born on 26 August 1691, but, possibly because of the Quaker influence within the family, he was not baptised until he was nearly 21.

His father was a blacksmith and, although Thomas (1) appears to have trained originally as a clockmaker, he also undertook small repair jobs in a more general field. His versatility can be illustrated by the fact that not only did the 3rd Earl of Cardigan employ him to clean and generally maintain the clocks at Deene Park, but also to supply hinges and bolts for the family pew in Deene Church, and to make and fit a lock to the Park gates. In 1726, the Earl employed him to cast a bell for the house clock and from then on Thomas (1) styled himself as 'bell-founder'. However, much of his work continued to be the making and maintaining of clocks; at regular intervals the Marques of Rockingham paid him five shillings (25p.) to visit Harrowden, (Northants), to 'Put in order and oyle the Clock'.

His son, also called 'Thomas' (2) joined him in the family business, and proved to be even more versatile, but, when *his* son, Thomas (3), inherited the business, following his father's death in 1761, it was already in financial difficulties, and he was obliged to sell up the household furniture to cover the debts.

In the Northampton Mercury of 22 March 1762, appears the following notice:-

'TO BE SOLD BY AUCTION
AT KETTERING, IN THE COUNTY OF NORTHANTS,

on Monday and Tuesday, 29 and 30 March, the entire HOUSEHOLD FURNITURE OF MR. THOMAS EAYRE, consisting of a variety of Beds, Feather Beds, Cabinet Work in Mahogany and Walnut-Tree viz. Drawers, Tables, Chairs, etc. Sconce Glasses, China Prints, Kitchen Furniture, and Brewing Utensils; a curious Spring Chime Clock and other Clocks in Cases, Barometers, Surveying Instruments and Peram-bulators. A neat Single-Horse Chaise, with Harness and Way Wiser (an instrument for measuring and indicating a distance travelled by road) as good as new. To begin each day at Nine O'clock.
N.B. The Bell-Founding, and Business of the Shops will be carried on by Joseph Eayre and Comp. of St. Neots'.

AN EQUALLY FAMOUS MAP MAKER

Thomas (2) who had made bells for churches in several other counties, as well as all over Northamptonshire, had many interests outside his work, including archaeology and antiquarian drawings.

Apparently, he got to hear that the Northamptonshire historian, John Bridges, who lived at nearby Barton Seagrave, was collecting maps, drawings and diagrams of the county's towns, houses and antiquities for his forthcoming 'History of Northamptonshire', (published in parts from 1762-1791). Eayre submitted some of his drawings for consideration, and must have been delighted when several of them (including a drawing of the Queen Eleanor Cross at Geddington) were selected for publication.

He also prepared some town maps for this publication, and, at a later date, he produced the first large-scale map of Northamptonshire. Because most of the surviving accounts which concern the Eayre family tend to include more than one item, it is difficult to put a firm figure on the charges that he made. However, it is recorded in the accounts of Loughborough church wardens that a Thomas Eayre was paid nearly £120 for recasting the whole ring of six bells.

Over 200 bells, in seven counties, have been identified as coming from the Eayre family foundry, and, although some have now been recast, there are still many which proudly bear the inscription 'Thos Eayre – Kettering'.

EMPLOYMENT IN THE TRAVEL INDUSTRY

Kettering's position on the main coach road between London, Nottingham and Leeds provided employment for many men, women and children. Not only did the large inns provide work for barmen, cellarmen, waitresses, bed-makers, laundresses, and cleaners, but also for ostlers and stablemen. In addition, several tradesmen in the town took advantage of the coach trade to help support their businesses. Amongst the receipts of the Kettering Coach Company are settlements made to the following traders:- E. Small and Sons – glaziers, 7 pence (2¾p) for mending the coach lamp with solder, and renewing the putty around a pane of glass. James Mingay – saddler, one shilling and nine pence (9p) for mending a coach strap and replacing it. James Maynard – Carpenter, was paid 1 shilling (5p) for mending a coach wheel and £3. 18 shillings (£3.90p) for a new set of 4 wheels, and J. Hindle, the painter, was paid 18 shillings (90p) for painting the wheels with four coats of yellow paint. The ironmonger (later known as Leach and Green) supplied an oil can for 1 shilling and 6 pence – (7½p) and six kegs for the same amount. Wheelwrights and blacksmiths were constantly called upon to repair wheels and to make and fit 'iron tyres'. Hay for the

KETTERING (contd)

horses was bought in at 8 shillings and 6 pence (42½p) per load, compared with £2 per bale at today's prices.

A typical receipt entered for payment by the coach-driver in 1808 was:-

Bed and breakfast at the Swan Inn, Bedford – 1 shilling and sixpence (7½p). Dinner – 2/6 (12½p), beer – 1 shilling and fourpence (7p).

VISCOUNT TORRINGTON VISITS KETTERING

The surviving diaries of the 17th and 18th century travellers not only give us a record the prices which the hotels were charging but sometimes a glimpse of their menus and the local tourist attractions.

When travelling south, in 1790, Viscount Torrington arrived at Kettering at 9.00 pm. His chosen inn, probably The White Hart, provided good stabling for his horse and a large comfortable parlour where he could spend the evening. As it was a summer evening, he supped with relish on a cold venison pastie and a side dish of cold roast lamb; the total cost being 1 shilling (5p)! After supper he walked in the market place and enjoyed the fresh smell coming in on the breeze from the nearby forest. He was up at 7.00 am, breakfasted on coffee and brown bread and went out to explore the town. He reported with great delight a visit that he made to 'Mr. Collis the stationer'. This gentleman had a well-known collection of fossils and stuffed birds where the Viscount spent some time before returning to the inn, saddling his horse and setting off on his way towards London.

THE VICTORIAN TRAVELLER'S GUIDE

Published in 1864 this book recommended The Royal Hotel and The George Hotel. It recorded that the population in 1861 was 5,498 and the chief trades were wool-combing and shoe making. This was undoubtedly true but they did not point out the very high level of unemployment.

PARISH RELIEF

Although some unemployed workers may have found unskilled jobs in the coach industry, the majority were left dependent on parish relief.

From the 16th century onwards, each parish church, at the Easter parish meeting, known as the 'Parish Vestry', elected two people to act as 'Guardians' and they were responsible to a local committee for collecting a 'Poor Rate' from each householder in the parish, and for distributing it to those people, who in the opinion of the committee, deserved limited help with their household expenses. This system worked very well during periods of high employment, but once the unemployment figures began to rise there was a strain on the working community. If unemployment rose sharply, then the strain could become unbearable, and in 1800 the Kettering Vestry Committee reported that the peak had been reached and that the rate was so high that rate-paying householders were so distressed that they were being pushed over the edge, and some were now asking for financial help instead of giving it! Help came from several different sources, but unemployment and the resulting financial distress continued. To try to keep people in work, the Vestry Committee negotiated with various firms to continue employing as many people as possible with the committee helping to cover the wage bill.

In practice, the committee could not really afford the money, and so the scheme proved too expensive. In 1820 they tried a more successful scheme. They started the 'Kettering Strong Linen Co.' On the 21 December 1819, the committee discussed the possibility of setting up a linen-weaving room. The plans went ahead and on 3 February 1820 they reported that money would be raised by a series of loans, with or without interest, at the option of the lenders. Just over £2,000 was raised, £500 of which was laid out in stock and £300 in yarn. On average, employment was found for fourteen active men and for six old men, women or boys. The wages bill for the first fifteen months was £676.

Although this project made a small loss, this was made up for by not having to give parish relief to these workers and their families. The scheme was continued and for some time twelve weavers and seven winders were given regular employment. A ready market was found for their work, which was of such high quality that the Kettering salesmen found shops in Lincolnshire selling Yorkshire linen marked 'Kettering Linen Company'.

THE FIRE BRIGADE

Another job for the Vestry Committee was organising The Fire Brigade. Not only Kettering, but many scattered towns suffered at this time from outbreaks of incendiarism. Following a quite serious out-break in September 1813, The Vestry Committee passed the following resolutions:-

(1) That the church wardens should put the fire engines into complete repair and apply to different Fire Officers offering insurance in this town, that they may subscribe towards the expense.

(2) That the church wardens should provide funds to pay 10 shillings from the poor-rate, twice a year, on Easter Monday and August 12, to enable 3 parish fire engines to be brought out for practice on these days.

This motion having been passed, the meeting was adjourned. They continued the following evening when it was agreed that an advertise-ment be place in the Northampton Mercury, offering a reward of 200

KETTERING (contd)

guineas for information leading to the conviction of the person/persons responsible for the burning down of Mr. Boddington's barley hovel on Tuesday, 28 September. This amount was subscribed as follows:- £50 from Mr. Boddington himself, £50 each from Sun Fire Office and Norwich Union Fire Office, and the remaining £60 from voluntary subscribers.

It was also agreed at the same meeting, that the church wardens, together with the Fire Insurance Officers' agents should immediately appoint 40 men to be called firemen and to fill any vacancies which would cause the force to fall below that number, for whatever reason. These firemen would receive, each Xmas Day, the sum of 2/6 (12½p), in addition to 2/6 each time they were called out, providing the property was insured.

On 2 July 1818 a report was published by the sub-committee appointed to look into 'the state of the workhouse'. Their main recommendations involved the sleeping arrangements in the building. Although 95 people were regularly sleeping there, only 48 beds were provided, many of which were unfit for use. It was decided that by combining 2 or 3 beds, perhaps one useful bed might be made, but that a quantity of new beds was absolutely necessary.

Lamport F9

THE FIRST PRESIDENT OF THE NATIONAL UNION OF TEACHERS

'THIS TABLET IS ERECTED BY THE
TEACHERS OF NORTHAMPTONSHIRE IN LOVING MEMORY
OF JOHN JAMES GRAVES
FOR 50 YEARS MASTER OF LAMPORT ENDOWED SCHOOL.
HE WAS FOR MANY YEARS AN ACTIVE AND
VALUED MEMBER OF THE
NORTHAMPTON AND DISTRICT TEACHERS ASSOCIATION.
ALSO ONE OF THE FOUNDERS AND FIRST PRESIDENT
OF THE NATIONAL UNION OF TEACHERS.
HIS DISINTERESTED AND LIFE-LONG SERVICES
IN THE CAUSE
OF EDUCATION GIVE HIM A LASTING
PLACE IN THE
HEARTS OF HIS FELLOW TEACHERS'.

John Graves was born on the 15 January 1832 and began his teaching career at an Anglican Charity School, St. Anne's, Soho, when he was only 14 years old. He showed great promise and the following year moved to assist at St. Paul's School, Cambridge and then spent a short time at Saleby in Lincolnshire. He was only 19 when he was awarded his first position as headmaster of the small Church School at Lamport.

This was one of the rural schools started by the Isham family. Sir Edmund, the 6th Baronet, made his will in 1758 and when he died in 1772 it was announced that he had left a bequest which would provide £15 per year to pay a schoolmaster and £10 per year for a schoolmistress, to teach poor children from Lamport and nearby Hanging Houghton. It was decided to build the school in the latter hamlet and as instructed in the will, staff were found to teach reading, writing and the casting of accounts. The girls were to spend less time on book-work and to be taught to knit, spin and sew. It was not always possible to get reliable staff, and, in 1762, the salary was raised to £18 and £12, and the staff instructed to add Religious Instruction and 'The care of morals' to their syllabus.

John Graves married before he arrived at Lamport, and he and his schoolmistress wife were provided with a house and a joint salary of £45 per year. His arrival coincided with the rebuilding of the school. Sir Charles Isham (who, with the local rector, was trustee of the school), provided a new modern building. There was a large room for the older children, with the desks arranged in three rows, eight foot deep, and thick red curtains were provided for dividing up the space. A second, smaller room was provided for the younger children and the whole building was heated by hot-water pipes – £5 per year being provided for coal.

For its time, this was a model school, and Graves had been carefully chosen for the position of headmaster. In 1856, he applied to the trustees for £2 to cover his expenses, so that he could attend a meeting of the newly formed Schoolmasters' Association. This was agreed, and he took an increasingly important part in this, and the Northampton and Northamptonshire Church Schoolmaster and Schoolmistresses Association. This Society was founded in 1846, with the aim of holding monthly meetings, to listen to lectures on the most modern methods of education, to witness demonstration lessons, and to share a helpful library. Graves would often walk seven miles there and back, along dark, muddy lanes to take part in these meetings.

Through the years he campaigned on several fronts. He wanted to make parents more aware of the benefits of education. He hoped to help them balance the possibility of better jobs for their children in the future, compared with their desire to lessen their present poverty by sending the children out to work. He called for more trained teachers, the legal insistence that no child should leave school under 12 years, unless they could prove they could read and write and, in addition,

LAMPORT (contd)

enough inspectors to see that the other points were carried out. He did his best to improve the situation by conducting night schools and encouraging others to do the same.

During 1853, he attended Shaftesbury Hall in London, to help form a group which became known as 'The General Association Body of Church Schoolmasters in England and Wales'. Four years later he was the unpaid Secretary.

During the year 1861/2, the Government, who were well aware of the terribly low standards in many of the elementary schools, brought in a new system whereby teachers should be paid by results. With his wide experience of education in Northamptonshire, Graves knew how disastrous this would be. How could teachers be expected to produce good results across the whole school, when such a large percentage of boys and girls were kept at home for days, sometimes weeks, at a time to earn money to help to support or care for younger children? Even if they were at school, how could they keep awake if they had been working late into the previous evening, either on farms or in the workrooms of the shoe industry? The most likely thing to happen was that the harassed teachers would cut out all the extra lessons that Graves had been encouraging them to teach, such as nature study and geography, and go back to concentrating on the 3 R's. Also, if teachers were all paid at one level, adjusted only by results, what encouragement was there for them to give up earnings, to spend time training as a Certificated teacher?

He himself was not certificated, but had earned a little extra money taking 12 paying pupils from outside the charity area, and these contributed an extra £20 to their joint unchanged earnings. An outbreak of fever in the school frightened these more distant parents, he lost this extra income, and was obliged to appeal to the Trustees. He pointed out that £30 per annum, or eleven shillings and sixpence (57½p) per week was little more than the full weekly pay of a farm worker, and that out of his wife's £15 they had to pay a child minder. From April 1859 their joint salary was raised to £60, and had reached £100 by 1880. He campaigned to help other teachers, and to improve the standard of education for many years. The first General Meeting of the National Union of Elementary Teachers was held at Kings College, London on 10 September 1870, when there was a call to unite together and forget the differences between teachers at Church Schools and Board Schools.

From then on, despite the death of his wife in 1882, and the continual expansion of his school (as parents slowly became aware of the benefits that could be gained by sending their children to a school where they could get a good, all-round education), he worked for the cause of an improved educational system, a more professional approach to the treatment of teachers, and a recognised salary scale with a pension to look forward to at retirement. By this time, the National Union of Teachers had been formed, with Graves as their first president. He made his closing address in 1900, and retired after 50 years at Lamport School, having seen many of the improvements for which he had campaigned, already established.

He lived on, with his second wife, until 31 January 1903 (when he was aged 71 years), and for the last two years of his retirement, enjoyed a pension of £20 a year.

Leighton Buzzard & Linslade

A COUNTRY TOWN

Thanks to the bypass and the street market, it is possible to imagine these two country towns as they were when livestock was still sold in the streets of the former (up until the 1930's) and when the Hunt Hotel provided stabling for 100 horses.

The Saxon descriptive name for Leighton was probably 'a village in the woodland clearing'. The suffix Buzzard was added by the Bishop of Lincoln's clerk when he had to collect rents from Leighton (Beds.) with a tenant called de Busar and from Leighton (Hunts.) with a tenant called Bromswold.

Linslade, across the River Ouse, was a separate Buckinghamshire town until 1965. In 966 when Edgar 'King of the English' bestowed it upon Aelfgifu, one of his relations whom he described as 'a noble matron', it was described as 'the land which the husbandmen of that province have given the ancient name "aet Lhincgelade".' (Lhin's glade or woodland clearing?).

Throughout the centuries, the valuable hunting rights were very carefully preserved. During the 15th century men were regularly charged in the manor court with poaching rabbits, hares, pheasants and partridges. At times this poaching was quite well organised – ferrets, spaniels, greyhounds, nets and traps are mentioned.

GROVE PRIORY FARM

From the time that written records began, Leighton was owned by the King but in 1164 King Henry II gave Lecton (Leighton) to the Nuns of Fontevrault, in France. Sometime before 1200 the Abbess of Fontevrault sent a group of monks to build a small monastery and protect her interest in the area. However, during the 100 Years War alien, or foreign, religious houses were unpopular and the Abbess decided to

LEIGHTON BUZZARD & LINSLADE (contd)

give Grovebury to Mary of Woodstock, sister of Edward II.
The bailiff's accounts for the year Michaelmas 1341 to Michaelmas 1342 are a valuable source of information for the mid 14th century.

1 gallon milk	1d.
1 whole Melton Mowbray Cheese	10d.
30 eggs for	1d.
hens	(each) 1½d.
capons	(each) 2½d.
geese	(each) 2½d.
swans	(each) 3s. 0d.
For paying rent – 1lb. pepper	1s. 1d.
For preparing pork – 1 bushel salt	4d.
For chapel light – 1lb. wax	6d.
For household light – candles	1¾d.
Bacon pigs	(each) 2s. 6d.
Peas and Beans	(per quarter) 1s. 8d.
Oats – sold at Dunstable Market	(per quarter) 1s. 10d.
Wheat – sold at Dunstable Market	(per quarter) 2s. 10d.

Wages

Carpenter	(per day) 2d.
Mowing	(per day) 4d.
Thatcher	(per day) 2d.
Female assistant – his wife?	(per day) 1d.
A carter – with own 2 horses	(per day) 5d.
Tiler and his lad – plus food	(per day) 2½d.
Gloves for harvest workers	(per pair) 1d.

N.B. These prices are very similar to those quoted for Harrold in 1308.
Some other items considered necessary for a house occasionally used by such an important lady:-
A pigeon-cote with 180 pigeons
1 pipe of cider plus 1½ hogshead still maturing.
Once a male heir had been born and was growing healthily, daughters were quite welcome because their marriages could bring not only money and land but also social advantages for the family. Although these girls were not necessarily married until they were 12 or 14, engagements were arranged while they were still very young.
Lady Mary of Woodstock died c.1338 and her daughter, Lady Maud, had inherited by the time that these accounts were drawn up. Maud's 10 year old daughter, Elizabeth, was already married to her young relative, Prince Lionel, the 2 year old son of Edward III!

RURAL INDUSTRIES

Not only did the farms and market bring employment to the town but so also did the coach industry of the 18th and 19th centuries and the wharves which were built alongside the river during the 19th century. James King and Son opened a Marine Store at Heath and Reach, Edward Lawford and John Osborn opened wharf offices by the newly-opened Grand Union canal (1800) and dealt in bricks and lime. The railway was opened in 1838 and in 1841, John Duke of Vandyke Road was already providing fencing and sleepers for the London and Birmingham Railway. Richard Lock in North Street and several other businesses in the town used local timber to make coaches; the landlords of The Swan Inn, Leighton Buzzard, and of The Railway Hotel (The Hunt), Linslade, not only provided accommodation for travellers but also their horses and specialised in keeping horses for hire.

One local industry led to another; Ann Webb straw hat maker in Church Square, Sarah Lock in North Street, Elizabeth Marlton in the Market Place and the owners of several other such bonnet sewing rooms were using locally-grown straw. Ann Collett in North Street, Kent and Wheeler in the Market Place and several other basket makers were using locally grown willow canes. Some of their baskets were specially designed to carry the local 'prune' plums by rail to cloth dyers in the North of England. Chiltern wool was sold at the Wool Fair, held on the first Friday in July and was stored in warehouses, near the river, before being despatched by barge.

The local white silica sand was sent by barge to the glass works in Wolverhampton but once the town began to expand to provide homes for all the people moving into the town to find work, both sand and the bricks made by Edward Lawford and John Osborn, were needed for house building. By 1841 James Saunder of North Street was already advertising as a builder, by 1876 he was joined by Henry Matthew Mead of Linslade. By 1881 the largest employer in the town was builder John Johnson who was regularly providing work for 170 men. A builder called Edward Dawson in Linslade was employing 24 men. Mr. R. V. Willis, who in 1984 published 'The Coming of a Town' recording, in some detail, the history and growth of the town, is the third generation of the Willis family, who in 1901 founded the building firm, now Willis Dawson.

Not only did the growth of the town fail to keep up with the demand for houses but at several times in the 19th century there were influxes of casual workers. Both the canal and the railway engineers were obliged to provide temporary accommodation for their workers but there were still many families looking for board and lodgings.

Also listed in the 1881 census was Henry Wilkinson, a coprolite contractor, employer of 120 men. A layer of Phosphorus nodules had

LEIGHTON BUZZARD & LINSLADE (contd)

been found in a long seam running from Cambridge across to Tring. Contractors recruited groups of labourers to dig them out, for conversion into fertilizer. They arranged their accommodation and moved them on from site to site.

LODGING IN THE TOWN

Several households in both Leighton and Linslade took in lodgers. In the later years of the 19th century people were so anxious to find safe and reasonably clean overnight accommodation that they were prepared to share rooms (and sometimes even beds) with workmates or even strangers. Consequently, providing accommodation for travellers or for people coming to work in the town was a good way of improving one's income.

A German gentleman, Augustus Gotzheim, whose main occupation was walking around the villages selling baskets, had a big enough house in Workhouse Lane to put up all 10 members of a German band. They were travelling across Bedfordshire with their brass instruments, playing outside public houses and on village greens.

A JOURNALIST'S MISTAKE

In its edition of 23 March 1869, The Bedford Times published not an apology exactly but a letter from a local solicitor. It was short and to the point. There were errors in the court news published in their last edition.
1) His practice was in Woburn not Leighton Buzzard.
2) He was representing the plaintiff not the defendant.
3) His client, Edward Saunders had sued John Giles and not vice versa.
4) Witness, Mrs Sanders is the sister in law of my client – not his mother.

Little Barford   M5

NICHOLAS ROWE

Most people who have taken an interest in the straw hat industry have come across the poem which Rowe wrote to illustrate how 'rural hobbies' had become a 'rural industry' and were socially no longer acceptable.

A Poetical Address To The Ladies of Bedfordshire:-
'Mama, it may be so
But then you lived full fifty years ago
Then you might safely turn the spinning wheel

And not be counted very ungenteel
But now the world much more polite appears
For fashions after in a round of years
Thus trade increases, the poor are daily fed
And thousands get their living by the head'.

Rowe was born in Little Barford on 20 June 1674, in his grandfather Jasper Edwards' comfortable manor house. He and his mother and father continued to live in this house until his mother died when he was four years old. His father, John Rowe, who was a successful lawyer, moved back to London where he remarried in 1687. Nicholas was a very happy scholar at Westminster School and around the time that his father died, when he was seventeen, he entered the Middle Temple. His father had left him an income of £300 per year and his chambers in the Temple so when he was called to the Bar on 22 May 1694 he was very comfortably placed. He married four years later and was soon combining a legal career with the profitable hobby of playwright.

His wife died within six years of their marriage and thereafter he devoted even more time to his work. For two years he was secretary to the Duke of Queensbury but when this friend also died he spent even more of his time writing and mixing with the other writers of his day, such as Swift. He was made Poet Laureate in 1712, when he was still only 38. Three years later he married again and he and his wife and their young daughter lived in a house in Covent Garden. At the age of forty-four he died, on 5 December 1718, and was buried in Westminster Abbey.

Long Buckby E12

A BUSINESSMAN – SHOEMAKER

Until the collapse of the cloth industry in the 1790's, this village, like many others, was noted for wool-combing and weaving worsted. It was left dependent on its local farms.

Even before the agricultural depression of the early 19th century, there was not enough farm work available to employ all the men, and by 1830 there was great distress. Thomas Lee, who was born in the village but had become a successful shoe manufacturer in Daventry, built a warehouse in the village, and from then on an increasing number of the young men were employed in making shoes. Some men did outwork, others worked in the factories, most did hand-sewing, but by the end of the century there was an increase in machine sewing.

During the 19th century, many shoemakers came and went, but one of the most colourful was William Sanders, who arrived in the village

LONG BUCKBY (contd)

during 1874. He had been born in Gloucester, and learned the skills of shoe manufacturing in Bristol, before emigrating to the United States of America. He returned to this country and opened a shoe shop in Liverpool, sailed back to America, returned to Liverpool, and then decided to settle down and make use of both his knowledge of skilled shoe manufacturing, (learned in Bristol), and his knowledge of the modern factory methods he had seen in America. The 'American' system of teamwork, whereby the part-sewn outwork was brought to a central point and finished by a series of workers, each highly skilled at his own job, was already established in Long Buckby.

Sanders took over a small factory which had got into financial difficulties, and re-opened it as 'The American Factory'. He took advantage of his experience in retailing and set up a chain of shops in nearby towns; then, with an American flair for publicity, started a brass band from among his employees, to be known as 'Sanders' Independance Band' and sent them to play in these towns to drum up trade. Another American idea which he used in his shops was to supply four width fittings within each size.

His success was probably due to his continued attention to the two precepts – quality of production and skilled marketing. His designs kept up with the fashions of the day, and he won prizes at the Frankfurt International Exhibition of 1881. At another level, he kept up sales by supplying a pair of half-soles with every pair of boots, and by sending out a travelling repair unit to save his customers the time and trouble of parting with their boots and shoes while they were sent for repairs.

Luton   H18

LUTON HOO

A family with the name 'de Hoo' was living on the present estate of that name before 1200. By 1247 a Thomas de la Hoo was of sufficient social standing to be appointed Bailiff of Luton when the manor was owned by the famous absentee landlord Simon de Montfort.

As the years went by, the family bought more land and greatly improved their financial and social status by marriage. The Robert de Hoo who was one of the MPs for Bedfordshire in 1294, 1295 and 1302, owned land in at least five counties. Luton and his other estates passed to his son, another Robert and then to his grandson, Thomas, in 1366. He married Isabella St. Leger, who added land in Sussex to the already considerable family estates.

This Sir Thomas took an active part in local and national affairs. He fought at the Battle of Crècy and helped to relieve the siege at Calais. As Sir Thomas atte Hoo he represented Bedfordshire in Parliament during the period 1366–1377. He died in 1386 and both he and his wife were buried in St. Albans Abbey.

The next Sir Thomas, who inherited in 1415, was the most famous member of the family. He became a prominent diplomat and soldier. As a young man he left Luton to become pageboy to the Duke of Exeter and fought with him in France, where he had a successful military career. He was later attached to the household of the Earl of Suffolk and in 1444 when the Earl was asked to undertake a delicate mission to France, to try to reclaim Normandy and at the same time to arrange the marriage of Henry VI and Margaret of Anjou, he insisted on taking a team of men who were both 'shrewd and able'; he chose both Thomas Hoo (who had been Chancellor of Normandy and France) and John Wenlock, who was described as the 'King's' squire.

Thomas Hoo was knighted and was given large estates in Sussex; he was put in charge of Hastings Castle and spent an increasing amount of time in Sussex. He had a successful political career, and, in 1448, was created Lord Hoo of Hastings. It was at Hastings that he died in 1455 and was buried in Battle Abbey. Luton Hoo passed to his four daughters, and the family name left Luton.

Although Baron Hoo married three times he had no male heir. His estates were divided between his grown-up daughter Ann, and three young daughters who were aged seven, five and four. Anna, the eldest of these three, grew up to marry Geoffrey Boleyn and many years later became the great-grandmother of the unfortunate Anne Boleyn, second wife of Henry VIII and mother of Queen Elizabeth.

THE CRAWLEYS OF CRAWLEY GREEN

The respected historian, William Austin, who is well-known for his books on the history of Luton, wrote a less well known book, 'The History Of A Family'. In it he traced the Crawley family's history from the 15th century, when several men of that name were farming small plots of land in the hamlets of Crawley Green and Nether Crawley. They also ascended in social position and wealth but, unlike the Hoo family, concentrated on farming and estate management and did not involve themselves in county or national affairs. However, as they became more affluent, they married the daughters of the landed gentry, and were able to educate their sons.

In the early 17th century, the Lord of the Manor of Luton was Sir Thomas Rotherham, who lived at Someries Castle, which he was anxious to sell. His neighbour, Thomas Crawley, was looking for a suitable property for his son Francis, who had qualified as a barrister at Lincolns Inn Fields. Whether it was a business arrangement (an

LUTON (contd)

arranged marriage) or based on a childhood friendship, we do not know, but Francis married Elizabeth, daughter of Thomas Rotherham and they moved in to Someries, bought for them by Francis' father.

Francis had an extremely successful legal career, becoming a judge in 1632, and being knighted by King Charles I. Both Sir Francis and his son Francis supported King Charles during the Civil War. He (Francis the elder) died in 1649 shortly after the execution of his king.

Several more generations of the Crawley family followed careers in the legal profession, mainly living in London. Someries was neglected, until in 1724, John Crawley sold the estate to Sir John Napier of Luton Hoo, after which it deteriorated rapidly. By 1740 John Crawley had completed a new house for his family in Luton, to be called Stockwood Park, where he and his descendants resided until well into this century. In 1945 the family sold it to the Luton Town Council.

The house itself has long been demolished but the stables remain, being used as a most attractive and interesting museum, while the extensive grounds are now open to the public, and a delightful walled flower and herb garden has been laid out as it would have been at the turn of the century.

Market Harborough   F7

Those readers who have an interest in horses and the many different forms of harness, which at different times have been used to control them, may have wondered about the history of the 'Market Harborough Rein'.

This additional running strap passes through the bit rings, and is attached to the normal rein by a small, metal hook, thus giving rather more control over an excited horse.

Although the original designer of this extra rein probably lived overseas, during the 1950's it was reintroduced by a man called Vickery who worked in the West of England. The numerous hunting enthusiasts who lived, or lodged, in and around Market Harborough, were so enthusiastic about this new form of restraining rein that they adopted it and gave it their name.

Maulden

A POOR BOY – APPRENTICED WEAVER

In the year 1695, it was a lucky boy who found himself in the position of being apprenticed to a craftsman. William Holmes was just such a boy. He had the good fortune to be apprenticed to Richard Beacham, a Houghton Conquest weaver. This placement was arranged by the two overseers of the parish poor, Ralph Kilby and John Ward, (the two churchwardens), and also with the consent of two Justices of the Peace. Apart from imparting the usual skills connected with weaving, Beacham also undertook to teach the boy to read the Bible.

William had to stay with Becham 'until he shall attain age of one and twenty years' during which time he was expected:- 'secrets shall keep, Lawful Commands he shall do' and 'hurt to his said master he shall not doe'. He was also prohibited from visiting Inns or Alehouses or 'play cards, dice or any other unlawful games'.

Beacham was paid £9, for which sum he was expected to provide his apprentice with everything he might need throughout the time William was attached to him. This included five suits of clothes, food, lodgings and washing facilities, and providing the craftsman kept to his part of the bargain, the young boy would have had a very valuable training.

Milton Bryan

THE MAN WHO DESIGNED THE CRYSTAL PALACE

Joseph Paxton was born in this village in 1801. Few gardener's boys can ever have grown up to live such an interesting and rewarding life. Son of a local farmer, he grew up and worked on the Woburn Estate and by the time he was 23 had been appointed head gardener at Chatsworth.

The Duke of Devonshire sent a message home, while on one of his foreign visits, that he was returning with a rare, giant, water-lily-like plant, which he named Victoria regia (now Victoria amazonica). By the time the Duke arrived home, Paxton had designed an enormous glasshouse which would cover the water and keep the plant free from frost. Under these extraordinary conditions the plant bloomed in Europe for the first time.

This vast structure became famous and when a competition was launched to find a design for a building to house the intended Great International Exhibition, Paxton's design, reputedly modelled on the

MILTON BRYAN (contd)

leaves of the famous plant, was chosen from the 250 entries.

Queen Victoria, who opened the exhibition, gave Paxton a Knighthood. Although he returned to Chatsworth, his whole life was changed, and in 1854 he was elected M.P. for Coventry and remained so until his death in 1865. He was buried at Chatsworth but there is a memorial window commemorating his life in Milton Bryan Church.

AN IMPORTANT PATH

A correspondent writing to the Bedford Standard of Friday, 10 April 1896, confidently predicted 'the approach of genial weather' because, on Good Friday afternoon a cuckoo had been heard in the trees on the path leading to Woburn Park.

This path was apparently very muddy and it was also reported that Mr. C. P. Hall (agent of Duke of Bedford) had agreed to have it cleaned and generally improved, because the historical associations 'of Milton and its beautiful church bring many strangers into the village in the summer months'.

Milton Ernest E6

A DOUBLE WEDDING AT ALL SAINTS CHURCH

On Tuesday, 6 April 1869, the two younger daughters of the respected vicar, The Rev. Beaty, were married in All Saints Church. Miss Amy married J. A. Price Esq. Capt. RA and Miss Edith married Marmaduke Althorpe Esq. BA of Corpus Christi, Oxford. These two young girls were very popular in the neighbourhood, so all the village turned out to watch and the churchyard path was decorated with 'tasteful green arches'. Over the entrance gate the local lace-makers had made an arch of lace which was their gift to the two young brides. The church was beautifully decorated with white tulips, heather, cinerarias and even azaleas which were sent by Lady Elizabeth Russell from Oakley House. Every seat in the church was taken and despite the crowds at the gate, the local reporter was delighted to record in the Bedford Times, that '. . . the most perfect order prevailed' and that there were 'no painful breaches of decorum'.

Northampton

THEY CAME TO NORTHAMPTON

Like all county towns, Northampton was visited by all manner of people poor and rich, clever and foolish, eccentric and downright dangerous. It was the Saxons who developed the present site and chose the strategically placed settlement as their 'Shire' or 'County' town. Life was very violent and the people of Northampton suffered several brutal attacks.

THE DANISH RAIDERS

The Anglo Saxon Chronicles report that in the days leading up to St. Andrew's Day (30 November) in the year 1010, the Danes came riding in from their settlements in East Anglia and destroyed Northampton by setting it on fire. Until King Edward of Wessex took control of the county in 920 they had used Northampton as their administrative centre.

Because Northamptonshire stands as a border between both East Anglia and the Fens, and the 'Heart of England', the Chiltern counties and the Midlands, leaders throughout history have found it a useful place for holding regional meetings and councils. Going back to the early years of the 10th century, the Danish invaders used Northampton as a centre from which to raid the towns round about. In 914 they rode

NORTHAMPTON (contd)

out towards Hook Norton (Oxfordshire) killing many men as they went. On their way back towards Northampton they joined up with another troop and rode on to attack Luton but '. . . the people of the country became aware of it, and fought against them and routed them completely, recovering all that they had taken and also a great part of their horses and weapons'. Seven years later they were still carrying out the same policy. Just before midsummer day they were confident enough to make a daylight attack on Towcester. When that town resisted their attack they reverted to night raids on villages and isolated farms, terrifying the area as far away as Aylesbury.

A DISCONTENTED SAXON EARL

Fifty years later, when King Edward, the Confessor, was on the throne of a loosely united England, Earl Tostig of Northumbria neglected his people so badly that they expelled him and planned to ask King Edward to make Morcar their new Earl. They marched down as far as Northampton and camped there while Earl Harold (Earl of

Wessex) rode to London and back to collect the official papers from King Edward, legalising the change of leader. During the time that he was away the Northumbrians and their supporters ran wild around the district killing, maiming and enslaving the people of Northampton and round about.

THE COMING OF THE NORMANS

However much the people of the county town resented the Norman Conquest, in 1066, they did not take up arms to chase out the new Norman landowners. King William I, known as 'The Conquerer' died in 1087 and both of his sons, William II and Henry I, had to fight off the challenge of their older brother Robert, Duke of Normandy. During the early spring of 1105, Henry I was staying at Northampton and his brother Robert came to him to negotiate peace terms and the return of his land, which Henry had captured in Normandy. These negotiations failed and Robert returned to Normandy.

There is no doubt that Northampton was a most convenient place to hold important national gatherings. In 1131 Henry chose Northampton Castle to hold a Great Council to settle the future of the English throne. On the night of 25 November 1120 a very large royal party had set out to sail from Normandy to England. The two sons of Henry I sailed on a new ship, owned by one of their father's friends, but it sank in deep water out in the Channel and both young men were drowned. Henry was left without a legitimate male heir and at the Great Council of 1131 he called all his church and secular leaders together, led them into All Saints Church and before the high altar they swore a vow of loyalty to Henry's daughter, the Empress Matilda, wife of Geoffrey of Anjou. It was an extremely unhappy marriage and at one time she was sent back to live at her father's court in Rouen. Geoffrey then sent messengers asking for the return of his wife and at the Great Council of Northampton, on 8 September, Henry and his advisers decided that she should be allowed to return to Anjou.

However, when just over four years later Henry I died, there was a dispute as to whether he had changed his mind, when he realised that he was dying, and named his nephew Stephen as his heir. While the argument continued in Normandy, Stephen arrived in this country and those church and secular leaders, who were resident in England, accepted him as king.

King Stephen held another meeting of the Great Council in Northampton on 3 April 1138 before crossing the country and attacking some Welsh castles which disputed his rule. On his way back to London he received messengers from Robert, Earl of Gloucester, illegitimate son of Henry I and stepbrother of the Empress, who had withdrawn his loyalty to King Stephen in favour of his sister. From the summer of 1138 the fortunes of war changed from side to side, and for a few months in

NORTHAMPTON (contd)

1141 King Stephen was in prison and the Empress Matilda ruled as 'Lady of England' but the English people turned against her and King Stephen was crowned on Christmas Day 1141.

During the spring of 1142, King Stephen travelled up to York to recruit more soldiers, but on his way back South he was taken ill when the party reached Northampton. He lay in bed, desperately ill, and a rumour got around that he had died of a fever. He recovered sufficiently to continue his journey but it was some weeks before he fully regained his health by which time Earl Robert was consulting with Matilda's husband, Count of Anjou. Stephen continued to march around the country, with his army, attacking Matilda's supporters and Earl Robert arrived back in England with her nine year old son, Prince Henry. The fighting was renewed and although Northamptonshire escaped the brutalities of war, the people suffered from shortage of food and other hardships. In 1144 there was fighting and great distress in Huntingdonshire and Cambridgeshire.

Stephen was back in Northampton in 1145 when Ranulf, Earl of Chester, arrived with a small band of his supporters to complain that the Welsh were attacking his property in Wales. He asked Stephen to mount a campaign against the border Welsh and it was only with difficulty that the King's advisers prevented him riding out of Northampton, abandoning his efforts to get complete control of England and taking his army to the Welsh Borders. Instead of which, Ranulf was imprisoned and Stephen gradually took back the castles that Ranulf had held. Robert, Earl of Gloucester, died at Bristol on 31 October 1147 and the Empress Matilda soon left England.

In January 1153 Matilda's son, the nineteen year old Duke Henry, arrived on the south coast with 140 knights and 3,000 foot soldiers. After several months, the two armies lined up at either side of the River Thames at Wallingford but their advisers persuaded them to back away and throughout the rest of the year, both armies roved the country causing desperate hardship and distress. Northampton was extremely lucky to be spared. Eventually on 6 November 1153 a settlement was signed making Duke Henry heir to the throne of England.

Stephen died of a sudden illness on 25 October 1154 and Duke Henry was crowned Henry II of England two months later.

THE KING'S ITINERARY JUDGES

During the reign of King Henry II, England was divided into six circuits of Justice and judges were appointed to travel around their circuits and hear cases which were referred to them by the sheriff of local magistrates.

Most of the cases that they dealt with concerned the ownership of land, matters concerning inheritance of land and property, especially if the Crown was likely to have an interest. Matters to do with the control of the Royal forests, estates, highways, or any matter thought to involve the exchequer were also discussed on these occasions, as were the 'Pleas of the Crown' such as murder, manslaughter, rape, robbery and any crimes involving the breach of the peace.

Some of the 17th century cases which caused most publicity were those of witchcraft.

WITCHES BROUGHT TO THE NORTHAMPTON COURT

As early as 1612, some 'Rare and Curious Tracts' were collected and printed by John Taylor, many of these concerned stories of witchcraft. They appear to be carefully researched and are so interesting that they were reprinted in 1967 under the title 'Witchcraft in Northampton'.

Joan Vaughan of Guilsborough

Looking back at these witch stories one can identify the common thread of an eccentric and maybe boorishly rude old lady who upsets and gradually alienates all her neighbours, until when the time comes that one or two of them join together and accuse her of the capital charge of witchcraft, the others do not interfere.

Agnes Browne and her daughter Joan Vaughan were two such ladies. Their ill-natured and self centred behaviour resulted in their being shunned and feared by their neighbours. One morning, when out walking near their Guilsborough cottage, Joan Vaughan passed Mistress Belcher, who was described by the neighbours as 'a Godly Gentlewoman'. Joan shouted out at her in such a vile, unseemly and impudent manner that Mistress Belcher was too annoyed to be frightened and slapped Joan across the face. It wasn't a serious blow but the stream of curses and threats that Joan threw at Mistress Belcher, caused her, despite her protestations of fearlessness, to hurry back home. Joan also went home and told her mother all about the incident. They talked it over for three or four days and then, we are told, came up with a suitable spell. Mistress Belcher woke up with an intolerable pain 'gripping and gnawing in her body'; she staggered about but returned to her bed with her face disfigured by pain. Her brother, Master Avery, was greatly distressed and when the neighbours came in and explained to him what had happened, set out with more 'rage rather than reason'. However, when he arrived at the cottage door, he was stopped by an invisible barrier. Day after day he tried to enter and finally realised that the devil was guarding the door.

He sent for the constable and for other strong men and eventually the two ladies were arrested and taken to prison in Northampton. Both

NORTHAMPTON (contd)

Mistress Belcher and her brother were sent for to scratch the so-called witches to see if they could draw blood – a scratch which didn't bleed being a sign that the person was a witch. The test was inconclusive and on the way home their coach was stopped by a man and lady, riding two black horses. The riders said that they had been sent with a warning, that either the couple themselves or their coach horses, would shortly drop dead. To their relief, a few miles nearer home, it was one of the horses that fell dead in the traces.

A few weeks later, both Agnes Browne and her daughter were cautioned and sent back home to Guilsborough where they gave further offence because they 'never asked pardon from man or God'.

The account ended with an even more bizarre postcript. Some time later the mother and daughter, together with a family friend, set out on a sow's back to visit another friend who was a known witch. They had heard that she was ill but were distressed to find they had arrived too late. However, the dead lady, Old Mother Rhodes, had left them a message. She had seen that they were on their way to visit her, apologised that they would arrive too late and promised to see them again in 'another place'.

Helen Jenkenson of Thrapston

This lady who was known, from time to time, to bewitch cattle, was accused in early May 1611 of causing the death of a small child. A brave lady called Mistress Moulsho accused her of the crime and arranged for other village ladies to help her search Jenkenson's body, for 'witch marks'. On her privy parts they found the evidence they were looking for and planned to remove her to prison in Northampton.

The next morning, Mistress Moulsho told her maid to hang the clean washing out on the line. The maid came screaming back indoors, several of the garments, especially Mistress Moulsho's own smock, were covered with daubs of colour representing toads, snakes and 'other ugly creatures'. Far from becoming hysterical, Mistress Moulsho was pleased, for now she really had evidence that her antagonist was working evil with the help of hob-goblins. Being of stout courage she visited Jenkenson and ordered her to instantly make the linen clean once more. Although her linen was indeed clean when she returned home nevertheless Jenkenson was sent to Northampton where she pleaded not guilty. Although the jury voted against her they could not force her to confess. Whether she was executed or died in prison is unclear.

THE WITCH FINDER GENERAL

The judges at Northampton were not the only ones to have to adjudicate when frightened or spiteful neighbours brought accusations of witchcraft.

In 1656, the county was on the edge of the area which suffered the attention of the self styled 'Witch Finder General'. This infamous man was only about 25 years of age when he started his crusade to search out and destroy witches. He was the son of the vicar of Great Wenham in Suffolk, trained in maritime law, but was never very successful as a lawyer. Then at the end of 1644, at which time he was living at Manningtree in Essex, he became convinced the the Devil was pursuing him and looked for a way of escape. A mission that would lead him towards righteousness. He knew that 17th century judges were quite prepared to convict on an accusation of witchcraft, it was just a question of carefully preparing and presenting the evidence. Gradually Hopkins decided that it was his mission in life to rid the country of witches. By the time he reached Northampton early in 1646, he had already been responsible for the death of over 100 men and women, in Essex, Suffolk and Norfolk. So exaggerated where his claims and so brutally cruel were his methods that by this time there was a strong movement growing against him and in June 1646, the Rev. John Gaule of Great Staughton published a small book entitled 'Select Cases of Conscience Touching Witches and Witchcraft', in which he warned that: 'every old woman with a wrinkled face, . . . a hairy lip, . . . a squint eye, . . . a scolding tongue, . . . and a dog or cat by her side . . .' was at great risk of being judged a witch. Probably because of this book and the numerous people who responded to it and rose against Hopkins' reign of terror, only three Northamptonshire people are known to have been imprisoned. A man called Cherrie, from Thrapston, died in prison, Anne Goodfellow of Woodford appears to have escaped punishment and the only person known to have been hanged was a young man from Denford. However, any odd or eccentric people living in Northamptonshire were lucky to escape. In the following year Hopkins was responsible for the death of at least seven men and women in Huntingdonshire and four, possibly seven, in Cambridgeshire.

CELIA FIENNES

Celia Fiennes was an amazing young lady who at a time when ladies seldom left their own village, without the protection of their male relations, and wouldn't be allowed to walk the streets of London without a servant in attendance, set out in May 1697 from her home at Newton Toney, near Salisbury, on the first of her great northern journeys. She rode side-saddle and was accompanied by two young female companions. They travelled up as far as Scarborough, keeping to

NORTHAMPTON (contd)

an eastern route via Peterborough and Lincoln and then turned south via Buxton and Warwick, entering Northamptonshire via Daventry, which she described as 'a pretty large market town and good houses all of stone'. When they saw the 'noble prospect' which lay a mile ahead of them they knew that they were approaching Northampton. They rode over a large bridge, where she commented that the 'water runs twineing about the grounds with rows of willow on each side of it which looks very pretty'.

She described the county town as:- 'a large town well built, the streets as large as most in London except Holborn and The Strand, the houses well built of brick and stone, very regular buildings; the Town Hall is new built all stone and resembles Guildhall in little; tho' it is a good lofty spacious place there is two Barrs in it with the benches and seat distinct, over one of the Barrs is King William and Queen Mary's pictures at length; the Church is new built its very neate, there is two rows of stone pillars at the entrance of the Church . . . there is abundance of new building which adds to the beauty of the town'. These new buildings were being built to replace those burnt down in the major fire of 1675.

Celia and her companions left Northampton on the road towards Stony Stratford. Their route taking them past the Eleanor Cross, many people have claimed to pinpoint which place is 'just in the middle of England'. Celia chose this cross. She does not realise that it is an Eleanor Cross (see above) and describes it as 'High Cross', confusing it with the one at Hinckley, although she realises that the four large niches each contain 'the statue of some queen'.

A DANGEROUS ROAD

Writing in the Gentleman's Magazine in 1747, a gentleman had this to say about the state of the road leading into Northampton:- 'In my journey to London, I travell'd from Harborough to Northampton and well was it that I was in a light Berlin, and six good horses, or I might have been overlaid in that turnpike road. But for fear of life and limb, I walked several miles on foot met 20 wagons tearing their goods to pieces, and the divers cursing and swearing for being robb'd on the highway by turnpike, screened under an act of parliament. When I got to Northampton I ran the gantrop thro' a number of soldiers to an obliging landlord . . . . I made my complaint about the bad road, and hoped that these lusty soldiers, according to the Roman usage and our methods in Scotland, were come to repair the highway; but was told they rather staid to prevent the country rising and cutting down the turnpikes, and to humble a rich town by living upon it'. He signed himself:- 'Scoto-Britannus'.

WRITERS IN RESIDENCE

Most county towns can boast that they have provided accommodation for at least a handful of authors. The two chosen here are completely different. Hans de Veil was a reasonably wealthy young man who arrived here from Holland c.1690 and studied at Cambridge University. He could then afford to settle in Northampton, study astronomy and publish at his own expense. John Clare, on the other hand, came from an extremely poor background, near Peterborough, gained his education from the village people with whom he grew up and only published his poetry with the greatest of difficulty.

Hans de Veil

King William III and Queen Mary arrived in England during February of 1689. The uniting of these two countries led to an interchange of students and scholars amongst whom was the young Hans de Veil. He became a student at Emmanuel College, Cambridge, passed his BA examinations and then decided to settle in the town of Northampton.

His main interest was in astronomy and in 1725 he published a pamphlet, under the intriguing title, 'An Essay Towards a Solution of the Horizontal Moon'. Twelve of the forty pages are made up of the dedication, which is to The Ladies of Northampton. He starts by explaining that:-

'In order to alledge some Reason why this minute Piece of Philosophy crowds itself under your Hoop-Petticoats for Shelter, twill be requisite to show the Connection between Astronomy and the Fair Sex . . .'.

He goes on to refer to ladies as stars and to the number of fair ladies in Northampton as exceeding The Constellations in the Firmament. He pokes fun at their hobby of stargazing, compares their eyes to celestial lamps and, daringly, draws a parallel between their bosoms and The Milky Way.

Then follows a story as to how twelve months previously he had fallen instantly in love with a Northampton girl he had met on the night of the full moon – gradually it becomes clear that this young lady is indeed Queen of the Moon and that he corresponds with her by attaching his letters to the string of a paper kite! In case his readers should lose interest, assuming that he has no time to spare for earthly females after consorting with the 'female inhabitants of the moon', he explains that the earthly ladies of his acquaintanceship are even more beautiful than those that he met in the moon. The latter suffering from attacks of mice! According to his story, the gallant Hans de Veil made a terrible mistake, he took a cat with him on his next visit, intending to rid the moon of mice. Instead of this, the cat caught and consumed 13 of the Moon-Queen's Life Guards thinking they were rats.

This adventure caused the queen displeasure but his next adventure

NORTHAMPTON (contd)

restored him to favour. The Moon-Queen's eldest son fell into a canal, when out fishing, and was near to drowning when de Veil came to his rescue.

Changing the subject he explains that the Moon-Queen's subjects now enjoy a cup of tea but that he finds himself unable to really appreciate it without the 'Dash of Scandal' that regularly accompanies it at home. However, he is sure it is only a matter of time before they copy that earthly habit as he has already taught them to cheat at cards.

The dedication continues along the same lines, gently poking fun at his earthly friends as he complains that he cannot persuade the Moon-Queen to wash her face with anything but water, nor can he persuade her grandmother to use false teeth. The ladies of her court refuse to have the vapours or to behave with their lovers in any but the most honest way, absolutely refusing to try the wiles of coquetry. Worse still, when kneeling at prayer, they close their eyes and utterly fail to look around the church and exchange provocative glances with the young men who surround them. Then, having assured them of his honest desire to please and interest them, he signs himself,

Your most humble Vassal,

Hans de Veil.

At last, after twelve pages of pure satirical whimsy, without any further explanation he then sets out what for the year 1725 was intended to be a sensible and scientific article.

The question of course arises, did the Hans de Veil who wrote the scientific article also write the introduction? The whole story is included in the second volume of Northamptonshire Notes and Queries where the editor points out the resemblance to the wit and satire which Swift used in Gulliver's Travels and which was published the following year.

John Clare

John Clare, who was born in 1793 at Helpston (between Peterborough and Stamford), was a sickly child and was removed from school at the age of seven to watch the sheep and geese which were put out each day to graze on the village green. There he met the old lady, known as 'Granny Bains', who helped him to pass away the long pastoral days by teaching him the old traditional songs she had picked up during her lifetime. As he grew older his health improved and he was able to work on a local farm, walking 4–5 miles each evening to study at Glinton School.

The landlord of The Blue Bell public house took an interest in the boy and when Clare was about 13 he was offered indoor work in the landlord's household and encouraged to study literature. This was followed by an unhappy period when he was in and out of work and consoled himself with writing poetry.

Completely by chance, in his 26th year, he used one of his old sheets of writing paper to enclose a letter that he had written to Mr. Drury, a Stamford bookseller. On this paper was the rough copy of his poem The Setting Sun. Drury showed it to a publisher who was so impressed that, in 1821 he published it in a volume called 'Poems Descriptive of Rural Life and Scenery by John Clare a Northamptonshire Peasant'. From then on, Clare's life went through several major changes. He was quite unprepared for the change in his social position as he was invited to meet the country landowners, London's wealthy patrons of the arts and other poets, artists and entertainers.

On the big country estates he was entertained in the servants' hall, where he felt perfectly at home, but when he visited his admirers in London, he felt out of place in their homes. At first he was shocked by the decadent behaviour of some of the artists and poets that he met but all too soon he was copying their wild behaviour.

His second book 'The Village Minstrel and Other Poems' published in 1821 was only moderately successful and later works, including his 'Shepherd's Calendar', were commercial failures. He had married in the Spring of 1820 and soon had a large family to support. Despite money settled on them by various patrons, they were desperately poor and by July 1837 his health, both physical and mental, was so unstable that it was obvious he would never again be able to hold down a job. However, he kept on writing poems even though they were never so popular as his early pieces based on rural life in north east Northamptonshire.

He was only 48 when, in 1841, he was admitted to the county asylum in Northampton. For another 23 years, nearly a third of his life, he lived there, and continued writing. He was well-known in the town where he could often be seen sitting in the sunshine.

Typical of the simple but observant poems that he wrote in his early years, is the 'Ballad' of the country girl, deserted by her shepherd lover. 'He had,
sought her out through frost and snow
When [her] apron did hang low'
But,
'When it puckered up with shame'
[She sought him out] he never came.

During his long lifetime he wrote around 2,000 poems, the majority of which were never published in his lifetime.

A HISTORIC HOUSE

There was once a Cistercian Monastery on the edge of this village but it was dissolved in 1537, passed to Henry VIII and when he died to his son Edward VI and from him to his sister, the future Queen Elizabeth. It remained royal property for many years until at the end of the 17th century it was bought by Samuel Ongley, who developed a country estate and played a large part in county affairs. In the village he sponsored new farming methods and built good cottages. In 1871, the year Lord Ongley sold the estate to Joseph Shuttleworth, an inspector described Old Warden as a 'model village'. The Shuttleworth family carried out further improvements: on some of the cottages you will see their gloved hand holding a shuttle.

THE SHUTTLEWORTH COLLECTION

The Shuttleworth family built the present house on the site of the old Ongley buildings and they also took part in county and local affairs. In 1889, Colonel Frank Shuttleworth J.P. was one of Bedfordshire's first county councillors. As early as 1824, the family had an interest in an engineering factory in Lincoln. They produced steam traction and ploughing engines. During the first World War they made aeroplanes including 'Sopwith Camels'. Between the wars Richard Shuttleworth collected and repaired old aeroplanes and motor cars. The latter took part in the London to Brighton Rally and the former flew in air displays from a small grass aerodrome at Old Warden. He joined the R.A.F. and in 1940 was killed in a flying accident. His mother Mrs. Dorothy Shuttleworth O.B.E. founded and endowed the 'Richard Ormonde Shuttleworth Remembrance Trust' in her son's memory. It is an educational centre 'for the teaching of science and practice of aviation and of afforestation and agriculture'. There is a Board of Trustees who manage the well-known agricultural college, the aerodrome, the estate and the fascinating Shuttleworth Collection, which is open to the public demonstrating transport history. There are old aeroplanes, motor cars, bicycles and a manual fire engine.

THE SWISS GARDEN

There is a story about the last Lord Ongley which may be based on truth. It is said that his young Swiss fiancée was caught in the garden during heavy rain, that she sheltered under an oak tree but caught cold and died. He had a 'Swiss' cottage built in her memory and a thatched roof put around one of the trees. There is a stone tablet nearby with a poem he may have written, 'The Forgotten One'. He moved away and the garden became overgrown. Voices were heard in the empty garden and people claimed to have seen a young lady in grey with golden hair.

The Shuttleworth family who at one time employed 28 gardeners, tamed the overgrowth, had the lawns mown and had a lady down from London to lay the ghost. 'The Grey Lady' has not been seen since but if you are very quiet you may see a deer cross the path! It is a fact that in the early 19th century Lord Ongley created a 'romantic garden' in eight acres of his grounds. This was developed around a 'Swiss' cottage which stands on a grassy knoll near the centre of the gardens.

During the last war the garden became overgrown and the buildings neglected. In September 1976, Bedfordshire County Council were assigned a long lease by the Shuttleworth Trust and have expertly restored the area, which is open to the public.

Olney A7

THE PANCAKE RACE

The name of Olney means different things to different people. Up until 1948 it was mainly associated with two famous hymn writers but during that spring, the vicar, Canon Collins discovered some old photographs of the pancake race, which had taken place in the town during the 1920's. He asked questions, looked up information in books and found that not only was there documentary evidence of the race taking place in the 17th century but also a strong tradition that took the race back to 1445. He formed a committee and on Shrove Tuesday 1948 re-established the famous race. In 1950 a challenge was received from the town of Liberal in Kansas, U.S.A. Since then the race has taken .place in both towns, the winner being declared following an international 'phone call. The press, radio and television companies of both countries became interested and since then the pancake race has become internationally famous.

THE COWPER AND NEWTON MUSEUM

Standing alongside the road, facing into the market place, is 'Orchard Side' a large house (originally two houses) which was given to the town by Thomas Wright. In 1900 it was decided that a permanent museum should be established to house the numerous pieces of furniture, books, music and other memorabilia which once belonged to the writers of the famous book of Olney Hymns, published in 1779. The museum not only has a John Newton Room and William Cowper Room but also a room devoted to local history and another to the history and social history connected with the local lace industry.

OLNEY (contd)

William Cowper

This celebrated poet was born at Berkhamsted Rectory on 15 November 1731. His mother died when he was only six and the young boy was sent to a boarding school where he was very unhappy. When he was 18 he went to London to study and spent some happy years with his cousins but in 1752 when he set up as a lawyer in the Temple, he began to suffer bouts of depression. However, they soon lifted and when he was free from the dreaded depression he was a normal sociable young man who occasionally wrote ballads for his own amusement and to share with his friends. As the years went by he was still troubled by depression, and eventually he left London and settled near Huntingdon. It was there he wrote his first hymns. During the summer of 1767, when he was 36 years old, the Rev. John Newton of Olney visited him with an introduction from a mutual friend. They recognised that they had much in common and a few weeks later Cowper and Mary Unwin, the widowed friend with whom he lived, moved into Newton's vicarage at Olney. In the New Year, Orchard Side was empty and they moved in. Although he had long happy periods while living at Olney and wrote not only hymns but the amusing and well-known ballad 'The Diverting History of John Gilpin', he still had periods of depression, and as Newton had left Olney it was suggested that he should move out to Weston Underwood. After only four years, in 1800, he moved again, this time as far away as Norfolk. He died on 25 April 1800 at the age of 69 and was buried at St. Edmund's Chapel in East Dereham Church. Several of his hymns are still in general use. The best known are probably 'God Moves in a Mysterious Way' and 'Oh! For a Closer Walk with God'.

The Rev. John Newton

As a young man John Newton went to sea and rose to become captain of a slave ship. He gradually began to dislike and then to thoroughly despise the slave trade. His Christian belief and routine Sunday observance suddenly changed; after experiencing a violent storm at sea, his belief became very real. He trained for the Ministry of The Church and as an evangelically inclined clergyman came to Olney, where he settled, and stayed for many years. He enjoyed writing hymns and was able to encourage Cowper. Newton's best known hymns are probably, 'Amazing Grace', 'How Sweet The Name of Jesus Sounds' and 'Glorious Things of Thee Are Spoken'. From Olney he moved to St. Mary Woolwich, London and stayed there until his death in 1807.

THE PUBLIC'S MOST OBLIGED SERVANTS

An advertisement in the Northampton Mercury, 4 July 1785, announced that:-
'THE OUNDLE AND THRAPSTON FLY' sets out from the George and Blue Boar Inn every Sunday, Tuesday, and Thursday Evenings at Nine o'Clock; and from Oundle the fame Evenings at Half past Nine, and arrives at the above Place at Two o'Clock. Performed by the Public's most obliged Servants.
G. SMITH and Co.
N.B. No valuable Effects will be accounted for above Five Pounds Value, unlefs entered as fuch, and paid for accordingly.

A PAULERSPURY CHARACTER

In the 1949 edition of Northamptonshire Past and Present, Wimersley Bush recorded his correspondence with the late B. J. Tomlin of Paulerspury.

When he was only two years old, the young Tomlin was left with both legs paralyzed. Anxious for his future, particularly his ability to provide for himself after their death, his parents bought him a field at Cuttle Mill, where he could keep a pony; they also bought a small cart so that he could drive around the local villages, selling groceries and other necessary goods. After deducting his expenses, he made about £4 a year, sometimes as much as £6. He described this way of life as 'a kind of paradise preciously to me'.

Then, in 1928, tragedy struck. An alteration was made to Watling Street, cutting right across his beloved field. The piece he was left with was of no use, as it was too awkward a shape for anyone to mow, either by hand or by machine. Although Tomlin Sen. had paid £170 for the field, his son only received £48 from the Council in compensation for his loss. He never recovered from this disaster and eventually he had to give up his pony altogether, getting round the village in a three-wheeled chair.

Bush ended his article by rounding off the story with an account of the death of B. J. Tomlin. After the death of their parents, his sister had moved in to look after him. It appears that, on a bitterly cold night in January 1936, when 'BJ' was about 70, and could hardly move without

PAULERSPURY (Contd)

aid even using his crutches, his sister was taken ill. He heard her call out but she was dead by the time he got to her. This happened at about one o'clock in the morning. He struggled to the door and crawled on hands and knees towards the house next door before collapsing at the gate. Eventually he was found, lying in the snow, and, despite the doctor's attention, he died the following night, in the lift, on his way up to the men's ward at Northampton Hospital. He and his sister were buried in the same grave at the Congregational Church at Paulerspury.

WHIT-MONDAY FESTIVITIES AT CUTTLE MILL

Apart from his own story, B. J. Tomlin remembered and re-told tales of happenings in his village in days gone by.

Every year, on Whit-Monday, at Cuttle Mill, the 400 members of the Sick Club would have a day of celebration, starting with a members' parade to the Church, where they held a service. Then to the accompaniment of the church bells, they returned to the pub, carrying their 5 foot club staff, decorated in red and yellow, and sporting three coloured ribbons. There they enjoyed a jovial and happy meal followed by dancing to the local brass band. Eventually the merrymakers would be dancing up and down the Watling Street, but if any traffic should dare to infringe on the merriment, the village policeman would stop the dancers while the offending vehicle passed through, and the party would recommence once it had gone by.

By about 9.00 p.m., most of the villagers were returning, happy but tired, to their own homes, so, after the playing of the National Anthem, the band would follow their example, playing 'I won't go home 'til morning' as they went.

110

HARVEST AT PAULERSPURY HILL

Before the advent of agricultural machinery, much if not all the work on the farm was done by hand. The workers were paid at different rates, and Mr. Linnell, the first tenant farmer maintained he could always tell at which rate the four men he employed were being paid. For 'if you are doing day-work, your wetstone goes as though it says – "Three roods and hardly that, three roods and hardly that" – but, if you are on piece-work, the whetstone goes – "a acre and a half and a little above, a acre and a half and a little above".'

At that time, the harvesting was done with a sickle, gathered with the left hand, and cut just below the little finger. If the haulm (the dried stalks or stubble) was wanted for thatching, the corn would be cut 8 in. from the ground and after the grain had been removed, the stubble would be mowed.

To provide work, when there otherwise would not have been any, the thrashing was done under cover in barns during the winter months. The work was done by the same regular workers, year after year. Two men worked on each Winnowing Machine, one standing at each end, and when, finally, the harvest was in, it was the tradition for all the men to sing:-

> 'Here we plow, here we sow,
> Here we reap, here we mow,
> Here we get Harvest Home'.

On hearing these words, it was customary for the farmer to present his men with a 'Hollowing Bottle', (which was like a beer-barrel, holding about a gallon of beer) whereupon they would take a drink each, repeating the rhyme, and so on, until the bottle was empty.

The other tradition that is still carried on in many rural villages today was the Harvest Supper. After this occasion, it was usual for the women to go gleaning, carrying the corn home on their heads, and later in the year thrashing the grain either with a stick or a thrail (flail).

A FAMOUS MISSIONARY

On the chancel wall of St. James The Great Paulerspury is a memorial to William Carey D.D. 'Shoemaker, Schoolmaster and Minister'. Born here on 17 August 1761, his family were well-known in the village, both his father and grandfather having taught at the village school.

He spent 41 years in India as missionary and social reformer while working as a Professor at Fort William Government College, where he translated various parts of the Bible into Sanskrit, Bengali and Marathi. He is internationally famous as founder of The Baptist Missionary Society. The memorial was erected in 1942 by the Northamptonshire Baptist Society, to commemorate their 150th year. He died in India on 9 June 1834.

Piddington J14

IN COMMEMORATION

The spire of St. John the Baptist, Piddington, was repaired during the winter of 1960-61. A tablet inside the church reminds us that the work was done as a memorial to those families who, in the past, had played their part in preserving the church for the present generation to enjoy. There is a particular reference to the familes of Rowe, Smith and Martin who have lived nearby for at least two centuries.

An oak tree was planted in the churchyard on 10 November 1974 by the first Hackleton Brownie-Guide Pack to commemorate the Diamond Jubilee of the Brownies.

Pitsford G11

A MEMORIAL TO THIRD BARON CHESHAM

Just outside the village, on the A508, stands a monument commemorating the life of Charles Compton, third Baron Chesham, who died in a hunting accident while following the Pytchley Hunt in 1907. The monument records that he was 'a good man, a gallant soldier, a true sportsman'.

Rockingham H5

CHESNEY WOLD ALIAS

In the years after 1846, when Charles Dickens had become a recognised author, he frequently visited his friends Richard and Lavinia Watson at Rockingham Castle. He dedicated David Copperfield to them and used Rockingham as his model when he was describing Chesney Wold, the fictitious home of Lady Dedlock in Bleak House.

'H. E.' BATES

Herbert Ernest Bates, known even within his own family as 'H.E.', was born in Rushden on 16 May 1905. Robert Lusty, writing in the Dictionary of National Biography, stresses Bates' quiet and reflective personality, his love of country walks, nature study and gardens but when we turn to the introduction of his autobiography, 'The Vanished World', and read about his childhood years in Rushden, we can see that his early years must, at times, have been very hard.

Childhood Memories

His parents, grandparents and family friends all worked in the boot and shoe industry and he lived in a comparatively poor and rough part of the town. He describes the street in which he lived as '. . . wholly of brick, not all red but ranging from plain white at the southern, more respectable end to a shade of dreary dreadful puce-blue at the other. There were two boot factories in that street and two more within sight of his house. His memories of Rushden in the first decade of the 20th century was of boot factories, bakehouses (few of the cottages had proper ovens) and chapels all woven in amongst the houses, with the pattern occasionally broken by a beer-house or sweet shop. As with many autobiographies, the author allows his mind to wander, and selects those aspects of his life which to him or her seem most interesting or relevant. Bates' own memories, backed up, he writes, by old photographs, bring to life the men who worked in the factories, with their long black cut-away jackets, their bowler hats or flat, almost peakless caps, boots on their feet, mufflers round their throats. At work their clothes were protected by long white aprons.

As a small boy he carried his father's tea into the factory. At that time the buildings were about 20 years old and he describes them as being three-storied, made of brick with heavy wooden front doors and windows made of thick, opaque glass. He went to school well before his fifth birthday and this must have come as a shock to the quiet little boy. His playmates in the street had filled his head with the horrors to be expected both within the school-room and the playground. When the dreaded day at last arrived, he put on a 'gigantic tantrum' only to be thwarted by the arrival of his step-grandmother. She completely ignored his protests, caught hold of his ear, and unceremoniously dragged him along the two streets between the safety of home and the unknown but easily imagined horrors of school, pulled him up the steps and deposited him inside the door of the local infant school. As so often happens, his

RUSHDEN (contd)

terrors were unfounded and after the first few weeks he was accepted by the unruly bunch of children and quickly learnt to read and write. Children's clothes, children's games, the struggle that some of their neighbours had in keeping the children clean, in dirty cottages which were lucky to have even cold taps in the kitchen, all these memories of his childhood in Rushden flitted through his mind as he sat in faraway Kent, putting together the first chapters of his autobiography. When he was 11, he moved on from the local school to Kettering Grammar School, having been awarded a free place.

His Love Of The Countryside

Bates was not a man whose autobiography would contain chapters of grateful memories concerning his old school and his schoolmasters. He credited his education and the two great loves of his life, books and the countryside (three if you include gardening), to his father and grandfather. His maternal grandfather, George William Lucas, was a highly skilled boot maker, in the days before machines were in general use, and lived at Higham Ferrers. As a young boy, Bates often visited him and there was a deep sympathy and affection between them. When the grandfather had been a young boy, he had worked as ploughboy on a farm and during the long and distressing period of unemployment, before the first World War, he left the boot industry and set up as a smallholder on five acres of land.

So, at the age of about five, Bates began to gain direct experience, not only of country life but also of the hard daily work of a smallholder, with too much work for one man and not enough land to make it economically possible to take on another. On those days when the weather was unsuitable for farm work, the old man and the young boy would set off with the pony and trap and explore the countryside of Northamptonshire and across the county boundary into Bedfordshire. So the young H. E. Bates grew up in an ambivalent world of dark and industrial streets on the one hand and the open, unspoiled countryside of the early 20th century on the other.

His father, who had had no choice but to spend his life within the world of boot making, had turned for consolation to music, books and country walks. As soon as his first-born son was old enough he took him out on ever-longer walks, unconsciously teaching him about the wonders of the countryside. Even before most people would have considered his son old enough, he almost, without thinking, taught him to read. While the boy was still very young he was encouraged to read the wide range of books on his father's book shelves.

He Begins To Write

Although Bates ended his years at Kettering Grammar School with good examination results he did not go on to further education. The one schoolmaster who made a serious impression on him was the English master, who joined the school when Bates was just 14. 'Write' he said '. . . from your own point of view'. Bates did just that, and knew that from then on it would be only a matter of time before he became an author. His headmaster suggested to his father that they should apply for a scholarship to Cambridge University but this was at a time when a scholarship would cover little more than tuition and a few books. Without a second thought Bates turned down the opportunity but he was sorry when his father then insisted that he should leave school and the world of books. However, his father was also adamant that he should avoid work of any sort in the boot industry and allowed him to wait for the right opportunity to come along. Meanwhile he earned his keep on his grandfather's farm. Just before his seventeenth birthday he applied for, and got, the position of junior assistant reporter on the Northampton Chronicle. The salary was ten shillings a week. Like all cub reporters, the most trivial, most boring and most time-consuming jobs eventually ended up on his desk. He accepted them all, he was writing and supporting himself – just, but the work was made intolerable by the editor and his alcoholic friends.

Rushden Hall

One gloomy evening, just as it was getting dark, he was sent to research a story at the Elizabethan mansion on the edge of the town, known as Rushden Hall. Writing his autobiography, more than 40 years later, he could remember the two great wooden gates, the big iron-handled bell-pull and the never-ending drive leading up to the front door. Entering the hall was like stepping into a refrigerator. Confused by the extreme cold the teenage boy, from the back streets of the industrial town, stood in the doorway trying to come to terms with the vast, wood-panelled hall and its numerous doors, draped in dark wine-coloured curtains. The details of the rest of that visit were soon forgotten, only his first view of the hall was etched on his memory.

Love For Lydia

A few weeks later, he was out on another story, when he saw a young, dark-haired and vivacious girl sitting alone in the back of an expensive car. She had to be going to The Hall and the memory of the smart car and expensively dressed young lady, against the background of the smoke-blackened buildings, was also filed away. It wasn't long before he left the newspaper office and unpleasant editor but sometime around 1950, nearly 20 years after leaving Rushden, he was mentally back in his home town. He wrote about a town with 10 chapels and 50 boot factories, a father who was a man of gentle and unargumentative temperament who loved music and an editor who 'looked like one of

RUSHDEN (contd)

those model porkers, fat and pinkish, squatting on his hind-legs with an advertisement for sausages in its lap : . .'. He added a girl with 'long coils of black hair that fell across her shoulders, so that she seemed to be wearing a hood'. She was in a car and he could only see part of her face and her raised coat collar; she was travelling to an old house with a hall where a draught of east wind, clear as a knife, whipped under the door.

These memories, knitted together, form the opening pages of his well-known book, Love For Lydia. However, this was far from being his first successful novel.

The Author

Soon after leaving the newspaper office he became a clerk, a position which left him with a great deal of free time. He was soon writing again with great enthusiasm, persevered and in 1926 soon after his twenty-first birthday, his first novel, 'The Two Sisters', was published. He married in 1931 and moved to Kent. During the war he was a Flight Lieutenant and at one time worked in Public Relations at the Air Ministry; this led to a series of novels based on the experiences of himself and his friends. Although his stories were pure fiction and his well-known characters grew as they went along into likeable heroes and loveable rogues, many people reading the Uncle Silas series can recognise places along the Northamptonshire/Bedfordshire borders, while others, reading 'The Darling Buds of May', can recognise places in Kent.

He was awarded the C.B.E. in 1973 and died on 29 January 1974.

Salford

GUARDIANS OF THE POOR

Until the Poor Law Amendment Act of 1834, charity was organised within each parish by two 'Guardians of the Poor' elected at the Easter Vestry of the Parochial Church Council. These Guardians were responsible for setting and collecting a poor-rate and for overseeing the way that the money was distributed. Where their books have survived, we can get an interesting picture of village life.

People searching for names of their ancestors will find lists of people either paying the poor-rate or receiving 'constant alms'. At Salford, for the four weeks ending 16 May 1829, 27 people (out of a population of 340 in 1831) received from 1 to 5 shillings per week. Their expenses are very revealing; examples drawn from the early 1830's show that they paid:-

Making two men's shirts	1s. 8d. (8⅔p.)
4 lbs. of beef	2s. 4d. (approx. 3p. per lb.)
2½ lbs. of mutton	1s. 4½d. (approx. 2¾p. per lb.)

Sandy · K8

R.S.P.B.

After starting its existence in Didsbury (Manchester) as 'The Fur and Feather Group' in 1889, the headquarters of the Royal Society for the Protection of Birds only moved residence to The Lodge in Sandy in 1961, five years after its first president, The Duchess of Portland, died. She had taken up office in 1891, the year 'The Fur and Feather Group' was renamed 'The Society for the Protection of Birds', and she remained as president until her death. The Society was granted a Royal Charter in 1904.

ACCIDENT ON THE ICE

The Bedfordshire Mercury of Friday, 16 February 1900 reported that Miss Alice Male, the nanny at Sandy Place, took Master Oliver Edgecumbe 'a bright, little fellow of eight years' and Kate Phillips, a young servant girl, to skate on a nearby pond in the park. To their horror the ice gave way and both girls slid into the water. The quick-witted little boy, who was still standing on the bank, managed to hold on to both girls and all three screamed and shouted for help. Allan Ball heard them, and ran to the rescue. Young Master Oliver, who was still quite calm, asked him to pull the nanny, Alice, out first as she was the heavier. Both girls were soon back indoors and were none the worse for their ducking.

Sharnbrook · D4

DESCENDED FROM A NORMAN OFFICER

A wedding announcement in the Bedfordshire Times during the summer of 1896 described the Right Hon. Lord St. John J.P. 16th Baron of Melchbourne Park, as 'Head of a family that came over with the Conqueror – in whose train, it is said, an ancestor was 'supervisor of waggons and carriages' during the invasion of England', (1066). The bridegroom, who was Lord Lieutenant of Bedfordshire, was about to marry 25 year old Miss Helen Charlotte Thornton.

RESCUE FROM FRANCE

Sir John Burgoyne, who was Lord of the Manor in 1870, was very fond of sailing, and kept his yacht at Ryde on the Isle of Wight. While he was anchored off Deauville in France, waiting for his wife to return from Switzerland, he was approached by a strange gentleman who claimed to be dentist to the Emperor, Napoleon III.

The Emperor's attack on Prussia had failed and it was feared that he had been taken prisoner. After some general conversation the dentist explained that the Empress Eugenie was hiding in the town and wanted to escape to England – would Sir John take her on his yacht? He was extremely doubtful but when his wife arrived she felt sorry for the distressed Empress and persuaded her husband to agree.

The Empress was disguised and smuggled on board. Terrified of being stopped, they slipped out of the harbour. Trying to behave in their usual carefree manner so as not to attract attention, they sailed as quickly as possible back to the Isle of Wight and unloaded their precious cargo. The Empress never forgot their kindness and returned to sail with them again under happier circumstances.

BOYS WILL BE BOYS

One of the many emotions, which do not change as the centuries go by, is the anxiety that parents feel when their children first leave home. As part of the Shefford Charter Celebrations, in 1975, Peter Harwood wrote a carefully researched 'Story of Shefford'. One cannot write about a town or village without writing about its people, and he includes some of his own family letters.

In the mid 19th century Thomas Harwood had two sons away from home, the younger having just gone to join his brother. This is part of the letter which Thomas wrote to them:-

'Dear Children

I write these few lines to you hopen to find you all well as it leaves us all at present except Eliza. She was taken very ill on Sunday morning but semes a little better this morning we have sent Williams box [his odds and ends and spare clothes left at home] by majers (Mr. Majer?) waggon and tell him to wright and let us no how he is giten on and how he likes is new place . . . . i hope you will see that he goes to som place of worship on a Sunday and dont for get your self for I shall whant you to be farther and brother . . . . . . and tell him i hope he will not be about the Street at nights for i know there is no good to be learnt there'.

MEMORIAL TO A CYCLIST

The small memorial garden at Girtford Bridge, near the original Great North Road, commemorates Frederick Thomas Bidlake who died in 1933. This famous racing cyclist, who joined the North Road Cycling Club in 1887, was not a native of Bedfordshire. However, he was at different times secretary and president of the club which began at the nearby Ongley Arms at Biggleswade; latterly the club owned a cottage at Eaton Socon. By the time that he died at the age of 66 years he had won over one hundred awards. In later years he was well known in that part of Bedfordshire as the official timekeeper and on his memorial it records that 'He Measured Time'.

Stoke Bruerne G15

PIONEERS OF THE CANALS

It was Francis, Second Duke of Bridgewater, (of Ashridge House over the Hertfordshire borders), who first employed James Brindley as engineer to plan and supervise his industrial canal to carry coal from his mines at Worsley in Cheshire to Manchester and other industrial towns. This took place around the year 1760. This proved extremely successful

STOKE BRUERNE (Contd)

and other canals were built in the North and Midlands. The Marquis of Buckingham commissioned a survey to see if it was practical to link the Midland canal system with London. In 1792, William Praed M.P. agreed to chair a committee to oversee the construction of this canal which had been designed by James Barnes of Banbury. There were terrible problems to be overcome; apart from excavating the actual channels, there were bridges, locks, lifts and tunnels to be designed.

Blisworth Tunnel

One of the worst problems which the engineers had to overcome was to transport the barges or 'narrow boats' across nearly two miles of hills between Stoke Bruerne and Blisworth. A 1¾ mile (2.8 km) tunnel was eventually opened in 1805 to the north of Stoke Bruerne and a series of five locks lowered the level of the canal to the south. The tunnel was a wonderful piece of engineering but it was not possible to build a towpath and take the horses through.

The Leggers

The horses were unharnessed and led over the hill, and two people, usually men, 'legged' (used their legs) to propel the boat through that great distance. On some small tunnels the boat owner and his wife could leg the boat through for themselves but at Blisworth the long, cold, smelly journey was usually undertaken by registered leggers who were hired from a hut beside The Boat Inn at Blisworth. They would lay on a plank and use the pressure of their feet against the side of the tunnel to keep the boat moving. At the far end they would cross the canal and wait for a boat coming in the opposite direction and hire themselves out for the return jouney. Their charge was 7½ pence (3¼p.) per journey!

The Waterways Museum

The Grand Union Canal passing through Stoke Bruerne is crossed by a typical bowed bridge, has the Blisworth tunnel on one side and locks on the other, so it is an ideal place to build a waterways museum. The opportunity came in 1963, just after the nationalised canals and navigable rivers had been brought together under the management of a new public body, The British Waterways Board. No longer were the canals considered to be a major part of the national transport system, and the colourful traditions and social history of canal life were in danger of being lost. A grain warehouse and mill formed the basis of the new museum, which stands across the water from the Boat Inn and there is a decorated narrow-boat on the canal beside it. The museum is visited every year by thousands of children, as well as adults, who are fascinated by the canals. It demonstrates the engineering work undertaken by Brindley and the other engineers, the important role played by the barges as they carried heavy goods around the country and the social life of the canal workers and above all the family life of the people who lived and worked aboard the narrow-boats.

Stotfold   M12

'FELONIOUSLY KILLING A SHEEP'

On the night of 16 October 1868, Jacob Brown, a labourer aged 18 years, was caught in the fields standing beside a dead sheep. He was taken to court and accused of theft; he claimed that he committed the crime while under the influence of too much beer. Nevertheless he was sentenced to eighteen months' imprisonment.

121

Sulgrave D17

AN AMERICAN CONNECTION

The manor of Sulgrave was once part of the scattered estates of St. Andrew's Priory, Northampton. Following the dissolution, it was sold to Lawrence Washington, who built a large family house where his descendants lived for the next 120 years.

In the church is a brass, commemorating the life of this Lawrence Washington, who was a wealthy wool merchant. By 1538, he had built up a large enough fortune to buy up several of the small agricultural estates in this area. He lived until 1584, when the estates passed to his grandson, Lawrence Makepeace Washington, and so to his great-grandson, the Rev. Lawrence Washington. His son, John, joined the army and in 1656 sailed for America, settled in Virginia, (in an area which became known as Mount Vernon), and founded the American branch of the family from which George Washington was descended.

The family coat-of-arms can be seen carved in a spandrel of the main doorway (and also carved on a stone tomb in Great Brington church, near Althorp). There are three mullets (stars) and two bars (stripes), and so is said to have influenced the choice of design for the American flag.

The manor house where the predecessors of George Washington (the first President of the United States) lived, was purchased by a joint Anglo-American Committee to commemorate 100 years peace between the two countries c.1914. It is supported financially by the National Society of the Colonial Dames of America and is open to the public.

Sundon F15

LADY OF THE BEDCHAMBER TO QUEEN CAROLINE

Charlotte, who in 1716 was wife of Sir William Clayton, Lord of the Manor of Sundon, was granddaughter of the Royalist leader, Sir William Dyve of Bromham. They did not live at Sundon and spent much of their time after 1727 in the household of the Prince of Wales, later George II.

Her husband was M.P. for Liverpool for some years before he bought the manor of Sundon and as he was a friend of the Duke of Marlborough, he later became M.P., first for New Woodstock and then for St. Albans.

Helped by the Duke and his wife, Sarah 'Jennings', he held several civil appointments and when George I came to the throne, Lady Sundon was made lady of the bedchamber to the Princess of Wales, Caroline of Ansbach. When the princess's husband became King, in 1727, Caroline was of course Queen and Mrs. Clayton was in a confidential and therefore powerful position at court. In 1735 George II raised Sir William to an Irish peerage, Baron Sundon of Ardagh.

Lady Sundon had many friends, some of whom were, admittedly, influenced by her confidential position as a personal friend of Queen Caroline. Her reputation had been somewhat tarnished by the bitter and 'catty' comments which Walpole included in his (published) letters. He once described her as 'an absurd, pompous simpleton' but this appears to have been on his personal dislike of her character. However, Lord Hervey, who also knew her very well, noted in his memoirs, that she despised '. . . the dirty company surrounding her`. . .'. He had noticed that she took great pleasure in helping people who were in no position to give repayment.

By the time of Queen Caroline's fatal illness in 1737, Lady Sundon herself was already suffering from what proved to be a terminal illness. She received a pension but her illness, which progressed until it was eventually diagnosed as cancer of the throat, dominated the last years of her life. She died on 1 January 1742 and her husband died ten years later. Their burial place was unknown until 1882, when workmen were repairing the floor of the Lady Chapel in St. Mary's Church, Sundon. As they removed the rotten boards, two coffins were revealed. Despite their public life at court, Lord and Lady Sundon chose to be buried privately in the church overlooking their own garden.

LORD SUNDON'S NOTE BOOK

There is a humble little book in Luton Museum in which Lord Sundon noted down some of his expenses for the year or two after he had bought Sundon manor.

'27 July 1716. Paid for my purchase of Sundon £8,388 16 shillings and 10 pence'.

As often happens one wishes that the notes were a little more detailed but his Christmas expenses, 1717, are of interest. His main present for his wife was £100 in diamonds! He gave his wife £125 to cover the household expenses over the festive period and sent £3. 4s. 6d. (£3.22½p.) to both girls' and boys' charity schools at St. James.

SUNDON (Contd)

FRIENDS OF JOHN WESLEY

At the time that Lord Sundon's executors were selling the estate, one of the yeoman farmers who held quite a large amount of scattered land around the village was William Cole. He and his wife became followers of John Wesley and invited him to stay with them when he was travelling in South Bedfordshire.

When he visited in 1757, Mrs. Cole had just received a large legacy. Whereas most visitors would have congratulated her on her good fortune, Wesley was concerned that the money would '. . . . drown her soul in everlasting perdition'.

The money helped them to acquire more land and eventually the family bought a house in Luton. It also helped them with their household and social expenses because William Cole was High Sheriff of Bedfordshire in 1757-8.

He invited John Wesley to preach the assize sermon, when the judge next visited Bedford. So Wesley returned to the county and preached on the text 'We shall all stand before the judgement seat of Christ'.

Sutton M9

THE DANGERS OF LEARNING TO WRITE

Although we may take it for granted that the '3 R's' are of great value, to both boys and girls, this has not always been the case. Until the Education Act, of 1870, few villages or towns provided weekday education for girls. However, the charity school provided by Burgoyne family bequests, in the late 18th century, appears to have taught both boys and girls to read. By 1840 the mistress, Mrs. Blythe, the rector's wife, was responsible for educating over 60 children. With help from various other people, she endeavoured to teach them all to read but she refused to teach them to write because she said that it was unnecessary for the boys and would encourage the girls to write home and spread gossip about their mistresses.

Toddington E15

THE VILLAGE PUB

Even villages which are divided by the main coach roads would have difficulty in claiming quite as many inns and beer houses as Toddington. Joseph Blundell, who wrote the definitive history of the village during the early 1920's, included the Ram, White Horse, Hare, Queen's Head, Red Lion, Waggon and Horses, Greyhound and New Inn as examples of those that had already closed and were being used as private houses or shops.

In 1581 Ralph Agas visited Toddington and made an extremely detailed map of the whole village. The castle mound stood much as it does today, the village green appears to be unaltered but there was a long narrow market place which ended a little way south of the village pond. Beside the pond stood, and still stands today, The Angel.

The Angel

Although The Angel is obviously a very old building, one of the first written records is when Rebecca, wife of Joseph Osborne, yeoman farmer, inherited it following the death of her father in May 1799. However, it appears that she immediately sold the inn to John Morris, at which time it was described as having 'the house of John Bishop on the south-east', and the house 'formerly of Mary Sutton, widow, to the north'.

The deeds mention that the landlord in 1801 was John Spufford and had previously been Thomas Chance. Although there have been many alterations over the centuries, much of the old inn is incorporated in the present building.

In a village which has so many different pubs each must create its own character. In 1984, Keith Baldwin, who had spent 15 years playing trumpet with the Eric Delaney and Ray McVay bands, together with his wife Paula, who was working as a freelance journalist and broadcaster, re-opened and renovated this important old inn.

They decided to develop the features of a traditional country pub, and also to create a centre where modern and mainstream jazz fans could hear their own particular style of music. There is a 17-piece, Glenn Miller-style Big Band which meets there regularly, and among the famous musicians who occasionally 'sit in' are George Chisholm, Bernie Fenton and Terry Lightfoot.

The Sow and Pigs

Along the front of the church, of St. George of England, is a cornice of grotesque animals carved from the local Totternhoe stone. Although the frieze contains a wide selection of birds and animals, as varied as a rhinoceros, a pair of peacocks and a mermaid, the village people insist that they represent a sow and her piglets which have given their name to the pub on the opposite side of the road.

Although the name goes back well into the 17th century, the present building was put up in the mid 18th century. In the manor court rolls of Toddington there is a note that Samuel Wells, who had been the

TODDINGTON (contd)

landlord of the Sow and Pigs since 14 July 1825, had recently died (early 1830's). Wells had left a will in which he instructed his sons-in-law, Robert Lindsell and William Hogg to sell his estate and divide the proceeds between his beneficiaries. Apparently this was done so that one branch of the family could keep the pub running and the other get his share of the value. William Hogg, together with Fred Hogg bought the pub for £740 on 31 July 1835. It then stayed with that branch of the family until nearly the end of the 19th century and these two men may be the ones who chose to replace the old building.

Toddington Poetry

Since the early seventies, until quite recently, the Sow and Pigs has been the home of that unique body known as Toddington Poetry. This was the brain child of the late Alan Harris. Alan, a distinguished educationalist working at the Open University and a no less distinguished poet, needed a venue for the expression of his passion for the writing, reading and hearing of poetry. The Sow and Pigs, a hostelry of singular character, was Alan's local. In no time at all he had persuaded the enlightened and cultured landlord, Roger Martin and his wife, Sue, that the Sow and Pigs would be the ideal venue for the meetings of those who loved poetry and good ale. Thus began Toddington Poetry – a society which was soon greatly respected. The society has given great pleasure, not only to local people but to lovers of poetry from counties round about. Many famous poets have visited the Sow and Pigs, including Dannie Abse, Alan Brownjohn, Peter Porter, George Macbeth, Adrian Henri, John Silkin, Ursula Fanthorpe, Carol Rumens, Wendy Cope, Gavin Ewart, Jenny Joseph, and many more. Douglas Dunn has come from Scotland, James Simmonds from Ireland, and John Ormond and Nigel Jenkins from Wales. All have expressed their gratitude for the privilege of being allowed to join in the fellowship which they found there.

Alan Harris tragically died in the summer of 1986. Roger and Sue of the Sow and Pigs needed the Upper Room for their growing family. It was no longer possible for Toddington Poetry to meet there on a regular basis as heretofore. Nevertheless Toddington Poetry still continues, albeit not in Toddington but at the Library Bar, Leighton Buzzard.

MR. PICKWICK VISITS THE SARACEN'S HEAD

As a young reporter on the *Morning Chronicle,* Charles Dickens travelled by stagecoach and post chaise all over the country. He spent one night playing bagatelle with other reporters in his bedroom at the White Hart, Kettering, and on another occasion, when he couldn't get home for Christmas, shared the landlord's festive meal of cod and oyster sauce, roast beef, a pair of ducks, plum pudding and mince pies. However, it was at the Saracen's Head, Towcester, that his Pickwickian characters had their adventures.

When Mr. Pickwick, Sam Weller and Bob Sawyer were returning from a visit to Mr. Winkle Sen., in Birmingham, they arrived at The Saracen's Head, Towcester, in pouring rain. Sam Weller persuaded his master to stay overnight. 'Wery good little dinner, sir, they can get ready in half an hour – pair of fowls, sir, and a weal cutlet; French beans, 'tatus, tart, and tidiness'.

Within ten minutes a waiter had laid the cloth for dinner and the friends were sitting by the log fire enjoying their meal by candlelight. Later having been joined by their acquaintance Mr. Pott they settled down, in their stockinged feet, to catch up on each other's news. Having neglected to mend the fire, they chose to descend to the warmth of the kitchen to enjoy a last cigar before bed. Opening the door to what they thought was an empty kitchen, who should they find sitting by the fire but Mr. Pott's rival, Slurk of the *Independent.* Mr. Pickwick was all for a discreet return to their own cold room but Pott 'pot-valiant' insisted on staying and the two reporters sat either side of the fire, each reading their rival's news sheets and noisily expressing their disgust.

As these remarks became noisier and more uncouth, the wicked Bob Sawyer deliberately enflamed the antagonists. Until Mr. Pott, of the *Eatanswill Gazette,* crushed the *Independent* beneath his foot, spat upon it and cast it into the fire. In return, Mr. Slurk of the *Independent,* took hold of his carpet bag, swung it in the air and catching Mr. Pott behind the ear, with an unseen hairbrush, knocked him to the ground.

Before Pott could retaliate with the coal shovel, Mr. Pickwick had managed to get between them, but so out of control were

TOWCESTER (contd)

the two rivals that simultaneously they attacked poor Mr. Pickwick who was only saved from serious injury by the quick thinking Sam Weller, who pulled a meal-sack over Mr. Pott's head, while the other two friends disarmed Mr. Slurk.

While Sam Weller helped his dazed master off to bed, the landlord escorted the two editors to their separate rooms and early the next morning on to separate coaches, allowing Mr. Pickwick and his friends to depart quietly for London.

TOM BROWN ENJOYS HIS BREAKFAST

Although the adventures of the young Tom Brown are also fictitious, the details of his first coach journey from The Peacock at Islington to his new school at Rugby are meticulous and obviously the result of Thomas Hughes' own experience.

He travelled in the care of the guard on the Leicester Tallyho; they left Islington at 3.00 a.m. and stopped at a wayside inn just before the 4th stage, for a hot drink and to give both Tom and the guard the chance to bring life back to their frozen limbs.

This may well have been at Markyate on the Hertfordshire/ Bedfordshire borders. It was an unofficial stop and Tom just had time to enjoy the new experience of hot purl* before he scrambled back on top and, wrapping his feet in the straw, was obliged to sit tight in the freezing dawn until they made their first official halt at half past seven; four and a half hours out of Islington. It was, therefore, not surprising that breakfast was quite a hefty meal.

The Saracen's Head at Towcester claims to be the inn where Tom enjoyed coffee, muffins and kidneys. He gives a detailed account of the dining room; describing it as a 'low dark wainscoted room, hung with sporting prints', with a blazing fire and a 'quaint old glass over the mantlepiece, in which is stuck a large card with the list of the meets for the week of the county hounds'.

Because many of the inn's customers were young men on their way to enjoy a day's hunting, the inn was already offering an enormous selection of food. On the sideboard stood a cold pigeon pie, a ham, and 'boiled beef cut from a mammoth ox'; on the arrival of the coach, steak, kidneys, bacon and eggs were brought out hot from the kitchen. There was bread or muffins, tea or coffee and for regular travellers, such as the coachman, a tankard of beer to wash it all down.

*Mixture of hot ale, milk, spirits, spices and sugar.

A FORTUNE IN DIAMONDS

One of Wellingborough's most famous sons was Sir Paul Pindar who was born c.1566. Although his family were prepared to arrange for him to go to university, he chose for himself a career in trade. His father was in a financial position to arrange an apprenticeship for him with a successful London merchant and at the age of eighteen he was already representing the merchant at his office in Venice. He worked well for his master, built up a business of his own and from 1609 to 1611 was consul for the English merchants at Aleppo. His diplomatic work was much admired and James I appointed him as his Ambassador to Turkey and then knighted him on 18 July 1620. By this time he had amassed a great fortune, part of which he converted into diamonds. In 1623, he was obliged to let Prince Charles take some of his most important diamonds, on the strength of a promise to pay at a later date. Another diamond, valued at £35,000 in 1624, he lent to King James I to wear on state occasions. Some years later, King Charles offered him £18,000 for this jewel. Pindar agreed but the payment was never made. Pindar was in an impossible position, Charles now owed him for diamonds which must have been worth nearly £100,000. In 1638 he had been ruling the country for nearly nine years, without the usual revenue provided by Parliament. He was desperate for money but he persuaded Pindar to obtain yet another diamond for him, valued at £8,000. The only return that Charles had been able to offer for all these jewels was the income as supervisor of the production of alum – Pindar himself having put up much of the capital to develop, together with a share of the income from administering the customs. Despite all this investment in the Crown, Pindar was still able to lend the exchequer something like £100,000 and, in 1644, during the dangers of the Civil War, was able to provide money to safely transport the Queen and royal children out of the country.

He returned home in 1623 but not to Wellingborough; he visited the town but spent most of his time in London at the house he had built in Bishopsgate. This was pulled down to make way for Liverpool Street Station, the 17th century wooden front being taken to the Victoria and Albert Museum. Despite all these transactions with diamonds, which must really be regarded as gifts, he gave at least £10,000 to St. Paul's Cathedral, paid for major renovations at St. Sepulchre's in North-ampton, gave extremely valuable silver plate to Peterborough Cathedral and All Hallow's Church, Wellingborough, and was still able to leave generous bequests in his will. The 'desperate' debts owed by the king and the exchequer were never repaid. Sir Paul Pindar died 22 August 1650 and was buried at St. Botolph's Church, Bishopsgate.

Whipsnade

THE FOUNDING OF THE ZOO

The main layout of the park is based on four avenues; the long one which runs along the ridge of the Downs, above the famous White Lion, is known as Escarpment Avenue and opposite is Central Avenue. Duke's Avenue, which commemorates the help given by the eleventh Duke of Bedford, links the Zoo Shop with the Escarpment, and Cut Throat Avenue runs from Wolf Wood down towards the tiger enclosure, on the escarpment. Where possible, the original field names were used for the paddocks and the name 'Cut Throat', is a nickname sometimes given to a small field used as a 'cut-through' or short cut. Other benefactors also have their names recorded; Lady Yule's Walk is the raised path overlooking the Brown Bear Pit, so named because Lady Yule, while the Zoo was still in the planning stage, gave £1,000 to pay for the Bear Enclosure and presented the Zoo with their very first inhabitant 'Teddy'. Miss Joan's Ride runs straight through the middle of the park. Joan Procter was a friend of Sir Peter Chalmers Mitchell, the man who inspired Whipsnade Park. She was Curator of Reptiles at London Zoo and during the early days when the Zoo was being laid out, she enjoyed a day in the country, riding to and fro across the park.

SIR PETER'S WAY

Sir Peter Chalmers Mitchell, the Scottish zoologist and journalist, was born in 1864. Having completed his education, he became a lecturer at Oxford University, moved to London and in 1903, at the age of 39, was elected Secretary of the Zoological Society.

With great enthusiasm, he set about raising money and introducing new features to the Society's Zoo at Regents Park, such as the Mappin Terraces. He wrote a number of books on zoological subjects and was created C.B.E. in 1918, and knighted in 1929. Much as he loved the Regents Park Zoo, he had a dream of a country Zoo where sick animals could go for convalescence. He also wanted to try keeping animals, from other climates overseas, in large paddocks in the English countryside. He and his colleagues searched for a suitable site within easy travelling distance of London, and at last they discovered Hall Farm, Whipsnade. Work started in 1928 and the park was opened to the public on Whit Saturday, 23 May 1931. It was an instant success. Sir Peter is commemorated by Sir Peter's Way which links the main circular road with the Hippopotamus Pools. When he died his ashes were buried within a stone monument in the park.

130

THE GOBLIN HUNTSMAN

During 1851, T. Sternberg published his collection of folk-stories about Northamptonshire villages. He was fascinated by the similarity of a local goblin story with the classical story by Boccaccio, 'Nastag and Traversari'.

In the early years of the 19th century, it was well-known that if, late at night, you wandered out into the nearby woods, you could hear the wild 'whoop' of the goblin huntsman, cheering on his hounds.

He discovered that the story behind this legend was that a gallant young knight once fell in love with the daughter of a gentleman ranger. She was famed for her beauty and coquetry, and while at first she was flattered and welcomed his attachment, she soon lost interest in him and he, driven mad by his love for her, plunged his sword into his heart.

So shocked was the young lady that she too died, and her punishment for dallying with his affections was to spend her spirit life being hunted by a demon knight.

HIGHWAY ROBBERY

On 12 January 1869 George Major of Holme Street, Bedford was out delivering groceries in the horse and cart belonging to his employer, Mr. Payne of St. Mary's Street. He was on the Turnpike Road between Willington Crossroads and Cople Tollgate when he was attacked by three men, one of whom held onto his horse's bridle while the other two pulled him from the cart. One of Major's dogs knocked down his assailant, while the other sprang at the man holding the horse's head. In the midst of the confusion, Mr. Mitchell, the baker from Great Barford, rode up and Major called out, asking for his help but Mitchell thought the men were larking about and rode on by. Nevertheless, the thieves were sufficiently frightened to grab Major's purse, which contained 6/10½d, and ran off without stealing his silver watch or causing further damage. When the case came to court, the judge reprimanded Mitchell for not helping to catch the robbers.

CELIA FIENNES VISITS WOBURN

When in 1955 the Duke of Bedford decided to open his house and grounds to the public, he was only reviving a custom which in the 17th century was taken for granted.

After Northampton and Stony Stratford, Celia Fiennes continued her 1697 journey south by visiting Woburn. In the days when ladies did no physical work and seldom, if ever, played outdoor games, exercise was very important. Even comparatively small estates had pleasure grounds laid out around the house with pleasant walks made of quick-drying gravel paths, winding round and round. Deer roamed in the park, just as they do today, and some of the small trees were trimmed into the shape of animals. There was a large bowling-green and eight arbours where bushes were neatly trimmed to provide shelter for the seats which were built within them; one seat was placed in a high tree, and was reached by climbing up fifty steps. Not only could one sit up there to get a bird's-eye-view of the bowls players and the pleasure grounds, but the ladies could sit up there to watch, while the gentlemen 'hunted' the deer which the beaters had driven round to a suitable position in the park.

WOBURN (contd)

The gravel paths provided for the ladies' walks, wove around the grounds and led to three large vegetable gardens. Celia was delighted to find that the Red Coralina gooseberries were ripe. They were large, thin-skinned and sweet, and she ate a great quantity. She passed under an arch and came out into a cherry garden (probably espaliers along the surrounding walls) and was amused to see that the bent old lady who was busy weeding was, in fact, a stone statue. When a long-time employee had retired, the Duke had ordered that her effigy should be built and dressed in her customary clothes. Whether it had been ordered to commemorate a lifetime of devoted work, as a bird scarer, or both, we are not told.

Still she walked on and passed to the other side of the house where she found more gravel paths and just as before they were arranged on several levels. If there was a break during a spell of wet weather, the house party could go out into the gardens and walk for a mile or more as they wound to and fro, up, down and around all these long winding paths. Below this tier of paths was a long narrow fish pond, another garden and a large shrubbery.

Woburn Sands   B13

WEDDINGS AT WOBURN SANDS

On Saturday, 29 July 1905, the whole back page of the Woburn Sands Weekly Messenger was devoted to an account of two weddings. On both occasions, St. Michael's Church was packed with guests and the many onlookers were obliged to wait outside. On Wednesday, 26 July, 'Miss Salmon was led to the Hymeneal altar by Mr. S. C. Hebard'. The bride was given away by her father, Mr. H. J. Salmon of Bury St. Edmunds, and was 'charmingly attired in a dress of white lace and orange blossoms'. Her attendants were her sister, Miss Evelyn Salmon, a friend of the same age and her young niece. The two older girls were in pink and the young one in white. They all three carried pink carnations, the young girl's being tastefully arranged in a basket. All three wore gold brooches set with pearls, their gifts from the bridegroom. The many female guests had 'charming toilettes' which added to the '. . . pictures-que character of the assemblage'. The service was fully choral and was performed by the Rev. D. W. Henry assisted by the Rev. E. W. Carpenter of Thorpe. 'As the happy couple left the Church they were assailed with showers of confetti . . .'. The wedding reception took place at the house of the bride's brother-in-law, Dr. Holmes. The assembled company drank to the health and happiness of the bride and groom and enjoyed a bridal cake and refreshments supplied by Mr. Norman of Bedford. No list of presents was available when the newspaper went to print but it was understood that they were 'both numerous and valuable'.

The following afternoon the Rev. Henry, vicar of St. Michael's, was back in church again, this time assisted by the Rev. R. A. C. Bevan (a relation of the bride) and the Rev. A. Hillard (High Master of St. Paul's, London, a relative of the groom). This time the bride was Miss Mary Roline Chichester Loraine Bevan, daughter of Capt. and Mrs. Bevan of Aspley Heath, and the bridegroom was Mr. Frederick Arthur Hillard, Headmaster of the Worcester Grammar School. Because the time was so short between the two weddings, the family had employed Messrs Laxton of Bedford to do the flowers. This bride wore a dress of white crêpe-de-chine and was 'accompanied at the altar' by four bridesmaids. 'This bevy of charming demoiselles formed a remarkably pretty picture, and each was attired in a dress of pink, relieved with mauve. They also carried bouquets of mauve flowers'. The Reception was held at the bride's home, after which the young couple left to enjoy their honeymoon 'in a quite up-to-date fashion, having decided to make a motor tour of the Thames Valley, and later in Scotland'. Over one hundred presents had been received 'and by the kind invitation of Mrs. Bevan, the tradesmen of the village, with their wives and families, were invited to a private view of the presents . . . an invitation which was taken advantage of by several, who thoroughly appreciated the privilege accorded them'.

THE SMALLEST NEWSPAPER

The Woburn Sands Weekly Messenger is thought to be one of England's smallest weekly papers. It was started by Herbert Gregory in June 1905, who kept it running for over a year from his office in the High Street. He charged one half-penny a copy. Number 7, quoted above, was headed as a Special Wedding Number. The whole paper was made up of a printed sheet (a little over A4 size) and was then folded to make up four sides, each of A5. The editor made no apology for devoting the back page to these two weddings, because he knew how popular such accounts were with his female readers. The front page had a picture of St. Michael's Church in the centre surrounded by adverts for four High Street shops. J. McMurtrie – House Furnisher, Henry Inwood – Tailor and Clothier, J. Elliot – General and Fancy Draper, and J. W. Tansley – Family Grocer. Page two was more than half taken up by the list of wedding presents, starting with emerald and diamond ring and set of Russian sables which the groom gave his bride and the pearl, ruby and diamond studs which she gave him. Many of the other presents were ornaments, cutlery, dishes, etc. made of silver. The rest of this page was

WOBURN SANDS (contd)

made up of an extremely brief reference to another wedding and a christening held in another village and advertisements for:- J. F. Smith – Sanitary Plumber and Glazier of West Hill, Aspley Guise and W. B. Toogood of The Bon Marché who specialised in ladies' hats and offered Black Chiffon Hats from 2 shillings and 11 pence, Ordinary Sailors from 6¾d. to 25/11d. and Trimmed Knockabouts at 1/6¾d. The facing inside page was taken up by an account of a cricket match, at which Woburn Abbey had beaten Leighton Buzzard by 225 runs to 66, and two more advertisements, the Post Office Aspley Guise, which also offered toys and fishing tackle and George Collins of Westbury House – Tailor and Habit Maker. The other half consisted of a serial story, suitably entitled, 'Love Story'.

INDEX – (PLACES)

137

138

INDEX – (PEOPLE)

141

Books Published by THE BOOK CASTLE

JOURNEYS INTO HERTFORDSHIRE: Anthony Mackay.
Foreword by The Marquess of Salisbury, Hatfield House. Nearly 200 superbly detailed ink drawings depict the towns, buildings and landscape of this still predominantly rural county.

JOURNEYS INTO BEDFORDSHIRE: Anthony Mackay.
Foreword by The Marquess of Tavistock, Woburn Abbey. A lavish book of over 150 evocative ink drawings.

NORTH CHILTERNS CAMERA, 1863–1954: From the Thurston Collection in Luton Museum: edited by Stephen Bunker.
Rural landscapes, town views, studio pictures and unique royal portraits by the area's leading early photographer.

LEAFING THROUGH LITERATURE: Writers' Lives in Hertfordshire and Bedfordshire: David Carroll.
Illustrated short biographies of many famous authors and their connections with these counties.

THROUGH VISITORS' EYES: A Bedfordshire Anthology:
edited by Simon Houfe.
Impressions of the county by famous visitors over the last four centuries, thematically arranged and illustrated with line drawings.

THE HILL OF THE MARTYR: An Architectural History of St. Albans Abbey: Eileen Roberts.
Scholarly and readable chronological narrative history of Hertfordshire and Bedfordshire's famous cathedral. Fully illustrated with photographs and plans.

LOCAL WALKS: South Bedfordshire and North Chilterns:
Vaughan Basham. Twenty-seven thematic circular walks.

LOCAL WALKS: North and Mid-Bedfordshire:
Vaughan Basham. Twenty-five thematic circular walks.

CHILTERN WALKS: Hertfordshire, Bedfordshire and North Buckinghamshire: Nick Moon.
Part of the trilogy of circular walks, in association with the Chiltern Society. Each volume contains thirty circular walks.

CHILTERN WALKS: Buckinghamshire: Nick Moon.

CHILTERN WALKS: Oxfordshire and West Buckinghamshire:
Nick Moon.

OXFORDSHIRE WALKS: Oxford, the Cotswolds and the Cherwell Valley: Nick Moon.
One of two volumes planned to complement Chiltern Walks: Oxfordshire and complete coverage of the county, in association with the Oxford Fieldpaths Society.

LEGACIES: Tales and Legends of Luton and the North Chilterns:
Vic Lea. Twenty-five mysteries and stories based on fact, including
Luton Town Football Club. Many photographs.

ECHOES: Tales And Legends of Bedfordshire and Hertfordshire
Vic Lea. Thirty, compulsively retold historical incidents.

ECCENTRICS and VILLAINS, HAUNTINGS and HEROES.
Tales from Four Shires: Northants., Beds., Bucks. and Herts.:
John Houghton. True incidents and curious events covering one
thousand years.

MURDERS and MYSTERIES, PEOPLE and PLOTS:
A Buckinghamshire, Bedfordshire and Northamptonshire
Miscellany: John Houghton. This fascinating book of true tales
roams around three counties and covers three centuries.

THE RAILWAY AGE IN BEDFORDSHIRE: Fred Cockman.
Classic, illustrated account of early railway history.

BEDFORDSHIRE'S YESTERYEARS: The Family, Childhood and
Schooldays: Brenda Fraser-Newstead.
Unusual early 20th century reminiscences, with private photographs.
Three further themed collections planned.

WHIPSNADE WILD ANIMAL PARK: 'MY AFRICA': Lucy Pendar.
Foreword by Andrew Forbes. Introduction by Gerald Durrell. Inside
story of sixty years of the Park's animals and people – full of
anecdotes, photographs and drawings.

FARM OF MY CHILDHOOD, 1925–1947: Mary Roberts.
An almost vanished lifestyle on a remote farm near Flitwick.

A LASTING IMPRESSION: Michael Dundrow. An East End boy's
wartime experiences as an evacuee on a Chilterns farm at Totternhoe.

EVA'S STORY: Chesham Since the Turn of the Century: Eva Rance
The ever-changing twentieth-century, especially the early years at her
parents' general stores, Tebby's, in the High Street.

DUNSTABLE DECADE: THE EIGHTIES: – A Collection of
Photographs: Pat Lovering.
A souvenir book of nearly 300 pictures of people and events in the 1980s.

DUNSTABLE IN DETAIL: Nigel Benson.
A hundred of the town's buildings and features, plus town trail map.

OLD DUNSTABLE: Bill Twaddle.
A new edition of this collection of early photographs.

BOURNE AND BRED: A Dunstable Boyhood Between the Wars:
Colin Bourne. An elegantly written, well-illustrated book capturing
the spirit of the town over fifty years ago.

ROYAL HOUGHTON: Pat Lovering.
Illustrated history of Houghton Regis from the earliest times to the
present.

THE CHANGING FACE OF LUTON: An Illustrated History:
Stephen Bunker, Robin Holgate and Marian Nichols.
Luton's development from earliest times to the present busy industrial town. Illustrated in colour and monochrome. The three authors from Luton Museum are all experts in local history, archaeology, crafts and social history.

THE MEN WHO WORE STRAW HELMETS: Policing Luton, 1840–1974: Tom Madigan.
Meticulously chronicled history; dozens of rare photographs; author served Luton Police for nearly fifty years.

BETWEEN THE HILLS: The Story of Lilley, a Chiltern Village:
Roy Pinnock.
A priceless piece of our heritage – the rural beauty remains but the customs and way of life described here have largely disappeared.

THE TALL HITCHIN SERGEANT: A Victorian Crime Novel based on fact: Edgar Newman.
Mixes real police officers and authentic background with an exciting storyline.

COUNTRY AIR: SUMMER and AUTUMN: Ron Wilson.
The Radio Northampton presenter looks month by month at the countryside's wildlife, customs and lore.

COUNTRY AIR: WINTER and SPRING: Ron Wilson.
This companion volume completes the year in the countryside.

Specially for Children

VILLA BELOW THE KNOLLS: A Story of Roman Britain:
Michael Dundrow. An exciting adventure for young John in Totternhoe and Dunstable two thousand years ago.

ADVENTURE ON THE KNOLLS: A Story of Iron Age Britain:
Michael Dundrow. Excitement on Totternhoe Knolls as ten-year-old John finds himself back in those dangerous times, confronting Julius Caesar and his army.

THE RAVENS: One Boy Against the Might of Rome:
James Dyer. On the Barton Hills and in the south-each of England as the men of the great fort of Ravensburgh (near Hexton) confront the invaders.

Further titles are in preparation.
All the above are available via any bookshop, or from the publisher and bookseller

THE BOOK CASTLE
12 Church Street, Dunstable, Bedfordshire, LU5 4RU
Tel: (0582) 605670